HOW ITALY
AND HER PEOPLE
SHAPED
CARDINAL NEWMAN

Jo Anne Cammarata Sylva

HOW ITALY
AND HER PEOPLE
SHAPED
CARDINAL NEWMAN

Italian Influences on an English Mind

NEWMAN HOUSE PRESS

COVER ART
Engraving, Cathedral of Milan and Piazza del Duomo,
in G. F. Rodwell, *South by East: Notes of Travel in Southern Europe* (1877)

Published in 2010 by
Newman House Press
601 Buhler Court
Pine Beach, New Jersey 08741

ISBN 978-0-9778846-4-3

Printed in the United States of America

EVERY step I took opened up a new world of joys, spiritual joys, and joys of the mind and imagination and senses in the natural order, but on the plane of innocence, and under the direction of grace.

There was a partial natural explanation for this. I was learning a thing that could not be completely learned except in a culture that is at least outwardly Catholic. One needs the atmosphere of French or Spanish or Italian Catholicism before there is any possibility of a complete and total experience of all the natural and sensible joys that overflow from the sacramental life.

Thomas Merton
Seven Storey Mountain

CONTENTS

ACKNOWLEDGMENTS

Finding John Henry Newman when I was no longer young has filled me with both delight and regret: I have had the joy of discovering an intellect and spirituality which have changed forever how I view my religion, and yet there is the disappointment that I did not know him when I could have used his sage observations to assist me with life-altering decisions. Now, thankfully, I know Newman, and, as he helped Gerontius, he has taught me to accept the rest of what God has in store for me in this life and beyond:

> *My soul is in my hand: I have no fear,*
> *In His dear might prepared for weal or woe.*
> *But hark! a grand, mysterious harmony:*
> *It floods me like the deep and solemn sound*
> *Of many waters.*
>
> —"Dream of Gerontius"

My road to Newman was a circuitous one. After teaching English for many years, I decided to enroll in Drew University to learn Italian, the first language of my father, a man whom I could not remember because he died when I was a baby. Dr. Daniela Bisello-Antonucci was my professor of Italian, who taught me much more than the words of my ancestors, for she introduced me to works of Italian literature which I had never known. With her encouragement and that of my beloved husband, Eugene Sylva, I entered the doctoral program, combining studies in the humanities with theology.

Once again, God's Providence was with me, as I took several graduate courses offered by the Very Reverend Peter M. J. Stravinskas, a priest and writer who became my mentor, editor, and friend. Just as Newman had a new and enriched life when he became a Catholic, so, similarly, did I feel this expansion of my existence when Father Peter taught me about Cardinal Newman. During my work for that course, I began to notice the several Italians who had assisted Newman in his life as he pondered Catholicism or once within the Church, and the idea for my future work began to evolve, a topic which attempts to bring a new understanding to these often-overlooked relationships.

As my research continued, I met other Newman friends, most notably the Reverend Nicholas L. Gregoris, a Newman scholar who helped me with the Italian translations, and Sister Josephine Vuochi, F.S.O., whom I met when I visited Little-more. Further, I thank my children—Mrs. Lee Anne Nugent, Father Geno Sylva, and Dr. Douglas Sylva, for supporting me in this project which has been such a labor of love.

Alla fine, mille grazie, Giovanni Enrico Neandri!

INTRODUCTION

Tradition for John Henry Newman was not just the development of Christian doctrine as a theological concept. According
to Monsignor H. Francis Davis, a former Vice-postulator of
the cause of Newman's beatification, "It was the Word of God
in our midst, bringing us eternal life, now as at all times in
Christian history. It involved the real presence of the Holy
Spirit and our response to that spirit. Tradition, Newman saw,
was bound up with the very process of being a Christian, provided Christianity was real. Do we, or do we not, live by the
Word of God in Scripture? How is this word that comes to
us in Scripture related to the Word of God handed down to
us by word of mouth? How is it related to the creeds we were
taught, and teach our children? Has our faith its roots in Scripture? Is it all on the surface of Scripture?"[1] Newman could
not have continued to live as a Christian without having answers to such questions.

The answers did come, and in many instances they came
from the people of Italy who as a group and as individuals
helped to clarify Newman's thoughts about specific aspects of
Catholic Tradition so that he would eventually come to comprehend that "genuine religious faith is a totally grace-informed
process of coming to see God as revealing and revealed."[2] Such
insights prepared the mature Newman to preach with conviction about Tradition as he did in his sermon for the Eleventh
Sunday after Pentecost, 9 August 1874:

---

[1] H. Francis Davis, "Foreword," in Günter Biemer, *Newman on Tradition* (New York:
Herder and Herder, 1967), xvi.
[2] M. Jamie Ferreira, *Doubt and Religious Commitment* (Oxford: Clarendon Press, 1980),
145.

If the Apostles were inspired when they wrote, and had the truths so clearly revealed to them, was their speaking not inspired as well? If not, their words might have contradicted their writings, all their teaching might have been a contradiction to themselves. Then it might be said: Why do we go by what the Apostles wrote and not by what they said? Their whole time was taken up in teaching, they spoke a great deal more than they wrote. Protestants will receive as the Word of God only what the Apostles wrote, not what they spoke, because they reject Tradition. By Tradition we mean this: giving over from mouth to mouth as it were—from father to son, what the Apostles spoke! Their teaching was like our catechism and we are to teach now what they taught.

Surely there are great advantages in writing; what is written can be handed over unchanged from generation to generation, and forms a steady basis to teaching by mouth.

Tradition makes customs pass into law.[3]

Yet, as Günter Biemer has said in his book *Newman on Tradition,* "It is, however, not easy to define which of the many meanings of tradition occur at any given point in Newman's writings. As an Anglican and as a Catholic, he often used the word in a wide, non-theological sense. Tradition or traditions can be historical with reference to general or to Church history, they can be cultural, juridical and political. . . . And finally there is the specifically theological tradition."[4]

The Italians included in this book—St. Alphonsus de Liguori, Blessed Dominic Barberi, Alessandro Manzoni, Antonio Rosmini, Giovanni Perrone, St. Philip Neri, and other Italians named and unnamed—all contributed to Newman's understanding of the many dimensions of Catholic Tradition. The specifically theological interpretation—the tradition of the records of the Faith in general, or, in a narrower sense, as oral tradition, which again can be dogmatic or liturgical—will be described as Tradition, while the wider meanings will be traditions.[5]

[3] John Henry Newman, "Excerpts . . . 9 August 1874," in Günter Biemer, *Newman on Tradition* (New York: Herder and Herder, 1967), 190–191.

[4] Biemer, *Newman on Tradition,* 167–168.

[5] See ibid., 168.

While the specific focus of this work is John Henry Newman and Catholic Tradition, it is more broadly a study in the awakening and eventual enlightenment in the mind of one of the most brilliant thinkers of the nineteenth century. These pages chronicle how "Newman allowed himself to be led into the fullness of Catholic truth" [6] by contemplating the unique grasp of Catholicism understood by many Italians. Further, he imprinted these beliefs into his mind and into his heart so that he would become more comfortable wearing the mantle of a Catholic priest and, ultimately, a cardinal.

---

[6] Paul Chavasse, "Foreword," in Nicholas L. Gregoris, *The Daughter of Eve Unfallen* (Mount Pocono, Pa.: Newman House Press, 2003), 14.

I

NEWMAN'S EARLY KNOWLEDGE OF THE ITALIANS

Hang that old monk Alfieri. A great fool writes tragedies, and is therefore jealous at anything sublime, for fear it should eclipse his own. A great fool of a monk dares to slander the high, lofty, magnificent fame of the high, lofty magnificent Virgil. [1]

With these words to his sister Harriet, the fourteen-year-old John Henry Newman made his first mention in writing of an Italian personage—one who was, according to him, a fool, a monk, and a slanderer. In Ian Ker's notes to Newman's *Letters and Diaries*, he adds: "Count Vittorio Alfieri (1749–1803), Italian tragic dramatist. He was not a monk." [2] However, young John assumed that since Alfieri was an Italian and a literary man, he must have been a Catholic cleric, and Catholicism was a Faith that, in his mind, meant mystery and incomprehensibility. This confusion was apparent in an early entry in his *Apologia pro Vita Sua:*

I was very superstitious, and for some time previous to my conversion [when I was fifteen] I used constantly to cross myself on going into the dark.

Of course I must have got this practice from some external source or other; but I can make no sort of conjecture whence; and certainly no one had ever spoken to me on the subject of the Catholic religion, which I only knew by name. The French master was an *émigré* Priest, but he was simply made a butt, as French masters too commonly were in that

---

[1] John Henry Newman, "To Harriet," 23 March 1816, in *The Letters and Diaries of John Henry Newman*, ed. Ian Ker and Thomas Gornall, S.J., vol. 1 (Oxford: Clarendon Press, 1978), 18. (Hereafter: *Letters and Diaries.*)
[2] Ibid., note.

day, and spoke English very imperfectly. There was a Catholic family in the village, old maiden ladies we used to think; but I knew nothing about them. I have of late years heard that there were one or two Catholic boys in the school; but either we were carefully kept from knowing this, or the knowledge of it made simply no impression on our minds. My brother will best witness how free the school was from Catholic ideas.[3]

Thus, by the age of fifteen, Newman knew as little about the Catholic Faith as he did about the French or the Italians. However, during this time he was to lose his state of religious uncertainty, for he had his first experience of a transcendent God. As he explained it, "A great change of thought took place in me. I fell under the influences of a definite Creed, and received into my intellect impressions of dogma, which, through God's mercy, have never been effaced or obscured. . . . I retained it till the age of twenty-one, when it gradually faded away; but I believe that it had some influence on my opinions, in the direction of those childish imaginations which I have already mentioned."[4]

Thereafter, for more than three years, Newman would not make mention in his letters of anybody or anything Italian, but with his conversion he seemed to gain a definite intellectual and spiritual maturity. When he next discussed the Italian people, it was with curiosity rather than disdain. In October of 1818 in a letter to his mother, he seemed excited to have been in a coach with two Englishmen who had recently traveled in Italy. He told his mother: "In Italy the sky is so clear, that one of them was at Rome during three winter months, and only one day was the heaven overcast with clouds. In the south of Italy they agreed with other accounts that the traveling is dreadful. One of them knew only three Oxford men who had ventured into the south, and all three returned stripped of their baggage."[5]

[3] John Henry Newman, *Apologia pro Vita Sua*, ed. Ian Ker (London: Penguin Books, 1994), 24. (Hereafter: *Apologia*.)

[4] *Apologia*, 25.

[5] Newman, "To my Mother," *Letters and Diaries*, 1:56.

Newman wanted to convey to his mother the idea that most English travelers had had disastrous trips in southern Italy and, further, that very few had even had the courage to make such a trip. Once again, the young Newman seemed to be interested in discussing Italy and, in this instance, in sharing information that he had learned about the country. However, this attitude of Newman that the Italian climate and countryside were most appealing and inviting while the Italian people, themselves, were most appalling and dangerous would remain intact for the next fifteen years of his life, until his first voyage to Italy in December of 1832.

Yet, further in the letter, Newman did tell his mother that those same men had enjoyed the Italian ecclesiastical music. He related to his mother what one of the English travelers had said: "To the lovers of music, there cannot be a greater treat than the *Miserere*—the Basilica Vaticana is filled with people mourning at the close of day—the sun descends, and the last taper is extinguished—there is a dead silence—the moon is observed rising and gleans thro' the window—the solemn chant commences in a low and melancholy voice. With that,' said he, 'I was affected, although I have no ear at all.' "[6]

The Prevailing Attitudes in England toward the Italians

Not surprisingly, young John Newman was conveying to his mother the conventional English attitude of their day—the Italians may have been outrageous thieves, but their music, like their weather, was sublime. According to Percy Young in his book *Elgar, Newman and "The Dream of Gerontius"*, the English appreciation for continental music started to develop almost fifty years before Newman's birth.

> With the death of Handel in 1759, an era in English music came to an end. Almost immediately a fresh impetus was given by the arrival in London—via Germany and Italy—of Johann Christian Bach and Karl Friedrich Abel—and by

[6] Ibid.

the cultivation of classical rather than baroque principles. It was no accident that it was during the period in which such principles developed that music assumed fresh significance in the only places of worship in England where Catholic church music could legitimately be performed. These, principally, were the chapels of the Portuguese, Sardinian, Bavarian, Neopolitan and Spanish missions. For fifty years, or thereabouts, these establishments enjoyed two-fold respect; on the one hand, for the pastoral facilities afforded to English Catholics; on the other, to a broader constituency on account of musical excellence.[7]

By 1782, as England gradually developed a taste for Italian music, the outlook for Catholics was also already more hopeful, and when worship no longer needed to be clandestine, the publication of appropriate music was timely.[8] One of the earliest and most profound influences on this music was Vincent Novello, the son of an immigrant Italian father and an English mother. Novello, an organist at the Portuguese Embassy Chapel, powerfully influenced English music in general but also insured that the English Catholic Church "would be able to fashion an independent order for its music, based on tradition, on European relationships, and on practicality."[9]

Like Novello, many of the singers employed in the Catholic chapels were Italian, and these singers were usually cognizant of the great Italian operas and, probably, of the traditional Italian church music. "At the time of John Henry Newman's birth, in February 1801, there was in England, a renewal of enthusiasm for an intellectual and aesthetic relationship with the European mainstream."[10] Thus, "a Catholic taste for music was notably part of the lives of many whose spiritual direction was similar to that taken by Newman."[11]

From all accounts, Newman's enthusiasm for music was apparent early, and he had his first violin lesson in 1811 at the age

[7] Percy M. Young, *Elgar, Newman and "The Dream of Gerontius"* (Hants, England: Scolar Press, 1995), 1.
[8] See ibid., 9.
[9] Ibid., 12–13.
[10] Ibid., 69.
[11] Ibid., 11.

of ten.[12] During those early years, the young man's musical and intellectual activity seemed endless, and in addition to playing the violin, he wrote verses, dramas, and operas (tunes and all).[13] It would not be so unusual, then, that the first Italian Catholic Tradition that Newman came to appreciate was the lovely music used in liturgical services.

In fact, in the same year that Newman first started to play the violin, Novello published a large collection of sacred music, much of it Italian. "Volumes containing works by Purcell, and by Carissimi, Clari, Durante, Jomelli, Leo, Palestrina, Pergolesi and other Italian composers . . . were to open doors to wide expanses of music hitherto unexplored in England." [14] In all probability, much of the music that Newman heard as a boy and as a young man would have been composed by or directed by Italians. In fact, in 1816, Newman's mother wrote of having gone with a friend to an orchestral concert at the King's Theatre, and the concert was directed by Signor Spagnoletti.[15]

The following year, John Henry Newman was off to Trinity College at Oxford where he was eventually to make many friends. Newman's letters to his family are the sole authority for his life at Trinity, since no reminiscences from other sources have been preserved. Once again, his main recreation was music, and his closest friend, J. W. Bowden, shared Newman's serious tastes in the subject. In addition, between them they edited an undergraduate paper, which survived only for a short time, and they published a joint composition poem called "The Massacre of St. Bartholomew." [16]

John William Bowden was a cellist, and the common love of music between Newman and him kept the two men in communication even after their undergraduate days. In a letter to his

[12] See ibid., 69–70.
[13] See Charles Frederick Harrold, *John Henry Newman* (London: Longmans, Green & Co., 1945), 5.
[14] Percy, *Elgar*, 14.
[15] Ibid.
[16] Bertram Newman, *Cardinal Newman: A Biographical and Literary Study* (London: G. Bell and Sons, 1925), 9–10.

sister Jemima from Oriel College in March of 1824, Newman
enthusiastically related what he had just heard from his friend
Bowden, and this most interesting topic happened to be music
and the Italians. Bowden had been present at a dinner in
Grosvenor Place during which Rossini (an Italian operatic
composer) had performed. Newman wrote: ". . . as far as they
could judge (for he [Rossini] does not speak English) he is as
unassuming and obliging a man as ever *breathed!* Only think, he
seemed highly pleased with *everything* and very desirous of making himself agreeable. Laboring indeed under a very severe
cold, he did not sing; but he accompanied two or three of his
own songs etc. in the most brilliant manner, giving the Piano
the effect of an Orchestra—no, *three* Orchestras." [17]

Newman was impressed by Bowden's description of Rossini,
and Newman related Bowden's enthusiasm to his sister. However, he also wanted to be certain that Jemima had a complete
picture of the Italians who had accompanied the composer to
England.

Newman continued his narrative: "As he [Rossini] came in a
private not a professional way, Bowden called on him—and
found him surrounded in a low dark room by 8 or 9 Italians, all
talking as fast as possible, who, with the assistance of a great
screaming *macaw* (o. th! [only think]) and of Mad. Colbran
Rossini in a dirty gown and her hair in curl papers, made such
a clamour that he was glad to escape as fast as he could." [18]

Newman seemed to be so interested in Bowden's professional and personal depictions of the composer that he had to
relay immediately the details to his sister. This description is
quite different from the one that he had written several years
earlier to his mother. At that time, there were no individual
portrayals of Italians—as far as the young man knew, they
were dangerous people who happened to live in a lovely climate and who produced beautiful church music. As a further
condemnation, they practiced a religion which was headed by

[17] Newman, "My dear Jemima," *Letters and Diaries*, 1:173.
[18] Ibid.

the Pope, and, at that time, Newman "was convinced that the Pope was the Antichrist predicted by Daniel, St. Paul, and St. John."[19]

However, by 1824, he had heard news of specific Italians; in fact, Rossini was described to him as a man of great talent and of gentle demeanor, albeit with an unkempt wife and noisy friends. One cannot help speculating whether this latter bit of gossip would have been transferred from Bowden to Newman to Jemima if the Rossinis had been an English couple! Nevertheless, one can see already in the eight years since Newman first mentioned Italians in his letters that he was starting to view the Italian people as individuals, and with music as the one common ground, he could appreciate them for their artistic talents.

Early Traditional Influences on Newman
    before He Came to Know the Italians

Tradition is basic to Catholic theology. According to the *Catholic Encyclopedia:*

> The word comes from the Latin meaning "handing over." In the religious sense, it is the teachings and practices handed down, whether in oral or written form, separately from but not independently of Scripture. Tradition is divided into two areas: (1) Scripture, the essential doctrines of the Church, the major writings and teachings of the Fathers, the liturgical life of the Church, and the living and lived faith of the whole Church down through the centuries; (2) customs, institutions, practices which express the Christian Faith.
>
> The Council of Trent (1546) affirmed both the Bible and Tradition as divine sources of Christian doctrine. Vatican II states, "It is clear ... that, in the supremely wise arrangement of God, sacred Tradition, sacred Scripture and the Magisterium of the Church are so connected and associated that one of them cannot stand without the others. Working together, each in its own way under the action of the one

---

[19] Harrold, *John Henry Newman*, 4.

Holy Spirit, they all contribute effectively to salvation of souls" (DV 10).[20]

However, Tradition within Anglican theology has always been difficult to assess. "Just as in the Protestant Church, where each theologian can put forward his subjective opinion in connexion with Sacred Scripture, without implicating thereby the doctrine of Protestantism, so too in Anglicanism important theological trends can diverge so radically that those outside may be left in doubt about the common doctrinal basis. . . . At the start there was no room for the doctrine of Tradition in Anglicanism. It was suspected of introducing unauthorized legends into the truths of Revelation and hence of corrupting Revelation by impositions and abuses."[21] Yet, in young Newman's time, antiquity, the Church Fathers, and the early Church were held in high esteem.

Newman, as a young boy, had a very great love for the King James Version of the Bible. "He is said to have read it from cover to cover before he was eight years old and even this early knew whole chapters by heart."[22] Through the Bible, Newman realized that there existed a revelation in which God had spoken of Himself and of His relations to man, and even before the young boy was capable of forming a personal judgment on the matter, he recognized Revelation in the "guise of Sacred Scripture."[23]

> When I was fifteen, (in the autumn of 1816,) a great change of thought took place in me. I fell under the influences of a definite Creed, and received into my intellect impressions of dogma, which, through God's mercy, have never been effaced or obscured. Above and beyond the conversations and sermons of the excellent man, long dead, the Rev. Walter Mayers, of Pembroke College, Oxford, who was the human means of this beginning of divine faith in me, was the effect of the books which he put into my hand.[24]

[20] "Tradition," in *Our Sunday Visitor's Catholic Encyclopedia*, ed. Rev. Peter Stravinskas (Huntington, Ind.: Our Sunday Visitor, 1991), 971.

[21] Günter Biemer, *Newman on Tradition* (New York: Herder and Herder, 1967), 5–6.

[22] John Moody, *John Henry Newman* (New York: Sheed & Ward, 1945), 6.

[23] Biemer, *Newman on Tradition*, 33.

[24] *Apologia*, 25.

In concrete terms Newman's conversion and his introduction to Reverend Mayers meant that he had experienced the existence of his Creator as an absolute certainty. "As a result of this experience, he felt himself from that day on to be unconditionally bound by the claims of God, and in particular to obedience. As this Creator speaking in his conscience was for Newman identical with the God of Revelation in the Bible, the principle of divine truth irrevocably laid down took possession of Newman's mind once and for all. Thus from his fifteenth year on, dogmatic truth became the fundamental principle of his religion." [25]

The early foundations of Tradition were beginning to implant themselves in young Newman's mind, but they were to be augmented by three theologians whom he would meet in the early years after he was elected fellow of Oriel College, Oxford, in April of 1822. "It was for instance Richard Whately, later Anglican Archbishop of Dublin, who had first taught him to look on the Church as an independent community, instituted by God, and so not tributary to the State." [26] "Whately stood out as the centre of a group, or clique, who had already come to be nicknamed the Noetics. Equally critical, equally ironical at the expense of High Church or Low (the former, Whately called the Sadducees, the latter, the Pharisees), the Oriel Noetics were to found a new party in the Church of England. Indeed, critical, aristocratic, and strongly attached to Tradition though they were, they were destined. . . to give rise to two new and divergent tendencies, the one Latitudinarian, the other Catholic." [27]

In addition, there was William James, and as Newman described his influence in the *Apologia:* "It is with pleasure that I pay here tribute to the memory of the Rev. William James, then Fellow of Oriel; who, about the year 1823, taught me the doctrine of Apostolic Succession, in the course of a walk, I think,

---

[25] Biemer, *Newman on Tradition,* 35.

[26] Ibid., 36.

[27] Louis Bouyer, *Newman: His Life and Spirituality* (New York: P. J. Kenedy & Sons, 1958), 58.

round Christ Church meadow; I recollect being somewhat impatient of the subject at the time."[28]

However, more importantly, it was from Edward Hawkins that Newman received an introduction to the specific doctrine of Tradition. "Hawkins was twelve years Newman's senior. As he was Vicar of St Mary's, he had perforce to remain in Oxford throughout vacation time, just as Newman was obliged to do when, shortly afterwards, he became curate at St Clement's. The pair of them, alone in hall and Common Room, could hardly help comparing notes, exchanging confidences."[29]

Hawkins had preached a sermon in 1818 on the "Use and Importance of Unauthoritative Tradition," which Newman had heard as a student. But he had not grasped its importance, its originality and its implications, since he lacked at the time the necessary presuppositions. As a fellow of Oriel and now to some extent a colleague of Hawkins, he was given the sermon to read in its published form. He studied it closely.

It starts out from the well-known text, "Therefore, brethren, stand fast, and hold the traditions which ye have been taught, whether by word, or by our epistle"(2 Thess 2:15, *A.V.*). Hawkins uses the form and structure of the New Testament writings, their unsystematic and to some extent allusive means of expressing themselves, to proceed to prove that Scripture can never be fully intelligible without aid and guidance. Such aid and guidance exist in the form of Tradition. Consequently, its existence is not due to the chances of history. It was foreseen by God and necessary. In other words, the usual and normal means for the transmission of the Christian Faith is in fact oral tradition. But Scripture then serves to indicate and prove the doctrines thus handed down. Remembering the impression which these ideas made on him, Newman was later to say that they opened up to him a wide field of research.[30]

However, it was through a book, and not through any direct personal influence, that Newman began to familiarize himself

[28] *Apologia*, 30.
[29] Bouyer, *Newman*, 61.
[30] Biemer, *Newman on Tradition*, 37.

with the school of Anglican Traditionalism. In 1825, the year of his ordination to the priesthood, Newman decided to read Butler's *Analogy*. As Newman stated the importance of Butler:

> Its inculcation of a visible Church, the oracle of truth and a pattern of sanctity, of the duties of external religion, and of the historical character of Revelation, are characteristics of this great work which strike the reader at once; for myself. . . it lay in two points. . . . First, the very idea of an analogy between the separate works of God leads to the conclusion that the system which is of less importance is economically or sacramentally connected with the more momentous system. . . . Secondly, Butler's doctrine that Probability is the guide of life, led me . . . to the question of the logical cogency of Faith, on which I have written so much. Thus to Butler I trace those two principles of my teaching.[31]

In fact, Butler was probably one of the first theologians to present to Newman the idea of the validity of oral Tradition when he said, "Nay, we are not in any sort able to judge whether it were to have been expected that the revelation should have been committed to writing, or left to be handed down." [32]

With his reading of Butler, the young John Henry Newman was gradually being exposed to some elements of Tradition, but, of course, in his mind they were consistent with Anglican theology which emphasized that Tradition was still not as important as Scripture. However, in 1826 after he was appointed a tutor at Oriel, Newman resigned his curacy and was back at Oxford where he would soon meet Richard Hurrell Froude, an ardent High Churchman.

> Newman had already come to know and admire another High Churchman, E. B. Pusey, who was elected a Fellow of Oriel in 1823, but he soon left Oxford to pursue his studies in Germany and even dabble there in liberalism.
>
> Froude was the disciple of John Keble, and between them they represented the old High Church tradition as its

[31] *Apologia*, 30–31.
[32] Joseph Butler, *Analogy of Religion*, quoted in Biemer, *Newman on Tradition*, 14.

noblest, but Keble, too, had retired from Oriel in 1823, to
assist his father in his country rectory at Fairford. Thus it
was above all through Hurrell Froude that Newman came
into contact with High Church beliefs, although it was
Froude's boast that his best deed in life had been to make
Newman and Keble understand each other. Froude was one
of the first religious Englishmen in the century to have a real
understanding and appreciation of the Roman Church. He
could not believe that Newman really considered it to be
under the influence of Antichrist. He regarded the Church's
Tradition rather than the Bible as the instrument of religious
teaching. He disliked the Reformers and his ideal was the
theocratic Church of the Middle Ages. He gradually made
Newman see the Reformation in a new light, and look with
sympathy towards the Church of Rome. Froude had a high
idea of the sanctity demanded of a Christian. It was he who
taught Newman to believe in the doctrine of the Real Presence, and to have devotion to the Blessed Virgin. Thanks to
Froude, also, Newman accepted the doctrine of the apostolic succession, that the Church and the Bishops derive
authority and power from their historic link with the Church
of Apostolic times. The old religious High Church teaching,
derived from the Anglican divines of the seventeenth century, thus reached Newman through Froude and Keble. But
they were the representatives of a very small party in the
Church of England.[33]

As Newman described this great influence of Froude—"He
professed openly his admiration of the Church of Rome, and
his hatred of the Reformers. He delighted in the notion of a
hierarchical system, of sacerdotal power, and of full ecclesiastical liberty. He felt scorn of the maxim, 'The Bible and the Bible
only is the religion of Protestants;' and he gloried in accepting
Tradition as a main instrument of religious teaching." [34] Thus,
it was no coincidence that Hurrell Froude, with his high regard
for the validity of Tradition in Christianity, would be the person
who eventually led Newman to Italy where he experienced,
first-hand, a people united in sanctity by Church Tradition.

[33] Charles Stephen Dessain, *John Henry Newman* (Stanford, Calif.: Stanford University Press, 1971), 9.
[34] *Apologia*, 41.

But, before Newman was ready to comprehend the Italians, he went through several other ordeals which would direct him towards a more spiritual grounding. "The truth is, I was beginning to prefer intellectual excellence to moral; I was drifting in the direction of the Liberalism of the day. I was rudely awakened from my dream at the end of 1827 by two great blows—illness and bereavement." [35] The "illness" to which Newman referred was an attack of nervous exhaustion which he suffered while being an Examining Master in November of 1827. Once before, when only a boy of fourteen, Newman had come under the influence of liberal ideas while reading Paine, Hume, and perhaps Voltaire. Once again, in 1827, a sickness in which Newman saw the ever-present guiding hand of Providence, intervened to save him.[36] "Now he discovered that the intellect he had begun to rely on too much was only an instrument, and could in a moment go horribly wrong, leaving him helpless. His mind was vulnerable; he had been relying on himself and his own powers—now sickness and death made him realize his weakness. It was a question of turning again from the world and the self to God." [37]

The bereavement of which Newman spoke was the death of his youngest sister, Mary Sophia Newman. At first Newman was totally devastated by the loss of this beautiful young woman who meant so much to him, but after time and contemplation he became animated by the thought of the past which belonged to him, and to him alone.[38] He vowed that "she 'shall flourish from the tomb.' And in the meantime, it being but a little time, I would try to talk to her in imagination, and in hope of the future, by setting down all I can think of about her." [39]

According to Father Bouyer, that concluding sentence was very revealing of what memory was to Newman. "It explains his

[35] Ibid., 33.
[36] See Thomas L. Sheridan, S.J., *Newman on Justification* (Staten Island, N.Y.: Society of St. Paul, 1967), 140–141.
[37] Meriol Trevor, *Newman: The Pillar of the Cloud* (Garden City, N.Y.: Doubleday & Co., 1962), 76
[38] See Bouyer, *Newman*, 105.
[39] Newman, "To My Dear Jemima," *Letters and Diaries*, 1:158.

anxiety . . . to glean, and piously to preserve the minutest details of the past. This anxiety remained all through his life a
conspicuous. . . feature of Newman's personality. But great as
was the importance he attached to it, it never suggests the sort
of embalmment of the past, as of something over and done
with, which is inevitable in the case of those who, unlike him,
cannot take the past as a starting point for the future. With
Newman, we cannot fail to recognize that contemplation of
the past is contemplation of the unseen. This fidelity to remembered details leads to fidelity to the person seen now no longer
in its mutable and transitory aspect, but in its eternal and
unchanging essence." [40] Newman's loss and his realization that
to remember Mary would be to keep her alive would also
predispose him to believe more and more that Tradition would
be a vital method of keeping a religion alive and vibrant for its
believers.

The shock of Mary's death, with all its after-effects, had prepared the way for yet another connection—a renewed friendship with John Keble. Up to now Newman's relations with
Keble had been purely external, but the cause of the great
change must have been the publication of *The Christian Year*, in
which Newman read several of Keble's poems. Newman was
much impressed with the pure serenity in which the whole work
was bathed. "And there is this to be added, it is poetry instinct
with a devotional quality that is quietly but very unmistakably
Catholic. That quality Keble had derived from his family traditions, which were not merely High Church but Non-juring. For
Newman, this was a discovery." [41]

There were also two main intellectual truths which *The Christian Year* brought home to Newman. "The first of these was what
may be called, in a large sense of the word, the sacramental
system; that is, the doctrine that material phenomena are both
the types and the instruments of real things unseen—a doctrine,
which embraces in its fullness, not only what Anglicans, as well

[40] Bouyer, *Newman*, 106.
[41] Ibid., 111.

as Catholics, believe about sacraments properly so called; but also the article of 'the Communion of Saints;' and likewise the Mysteries of the Faith." [42]

"On the second intellectual principle which I gained from Mr. Keble, I could say a great deal; if this were the place for it. ... In matters of religion, he seemed to say, it is not merely probability which makes us intellectually certain, but probability as it is put to account by faith and love. It is faith and love which give to probability a force which it has not in itself. Faith and love are directed towards an Object; in the vision of that Object they live; it is that Object, received in faith and love, which renders it reasonable to take probability as sufficient for internal conviction. Thus the argument from Probability, in the matter of religion, became an argument from Personality, which in fact is one form of the argument from Authority." [43]

In addition to reading Keble's *The Christian Year*, Newman also decided to return to his study of the Fathers. "Newman now took advantage of Pusey's second Continental visit to ask him to buy and send him the best available editions. On the 18th October, 1827, he writes to his mother telling her of their arrival: 'My Fathers are arrived all safe—huge fellows they are, but very cheap—one folio costs a shilling! And all in this extravagantly moderate way.' These volumes which invaded his modest quarters at Oriel were always kept together, and they remained all in a row at Birmingham, where he installed them after the foundation of the Oratory. They are for the most part splendid Benedictine editions of the seventeenth century." [44]

Newman was deeply affected by his reading of the Fathers, but it had taken the upheaval of the winter of 1827–1828, and, in particular, the thoughts and sadness brought out by Mary's death, to bring into full view a vision which till then had been enshrouded in twilight. "Newman was certainly well endowed with gifts that fitted him to be the Seer as well as the Poet of the

[42] *Apologia*, 37.
[43] *Apologia*, 37–38.
[44] Bouyer, *Newman*, 112.

Invisible. But he possessed in equal measure the gifts of the critic and the dialectician. If his patristic studies were destined to advance the former at the expense of the latter, the events of that sorrowful year played a large and providential part in contributing to that result. Now the die was cast; his path was chosen. His sermons . . . were soon to bear this out. The call to holiness rather than to peace becomes ever clearer and more insistent in them. Trusting in the vision of that invisible world which lies beyond the world we see, Newman exhorts us ever more and more to look beyond this latter, so that we may come at length, in the words he chose for his epitaph, *ex umbris et imaginibus in veritatem.*" [45]

But at this point in his life, John Newman was not truly ready to come out of the shadows. He was a greatly overworked man, and he was in a mental conflict over the struggle for Catholic emancipation. This issue had been in the air for over twenty years, and with the election in 1828 of an Irish Catholic to the House of Commons, the then-prime minister and his home secretary, Robert Peel, felt that Catholic Emancipation was necessary in order to avoid civil war in Ireland. "But Peel, having taken office committed against such a move, felt honor-bound to resign his position in Parliament and stand again for his seat. It was the seat from Oxford. A bitter contest followed, with the various dons choosing sides for the election. The liberals, led by Hawkins . . . together with Pusey, were leading the campaign for Peel's re-election. But Newman swung to the other side, and supported the movement to block Peel's re-election." [46] As Newman explained his position to his mother:

> All these things being considered, I am clearly in *principle* an Anti-Catholic; and, if I do not oppose the Emancipation, it is only because I do not think it expedient, perhaps possible, so to do. I do not look for the settlement of difficulties by the measure, they are rather begun by it, and will be settled with the downfall of the Established Church. If then I am for

---

[45] Ibid., 115.
[46] Gary Lease, *Witness to the Faith* (Pittsburgh: Duquesne University Press, 1971), 7.

Emancipation, it is only that I may take my stand against the foes of the Church on better ground, instead of fighting at a disadvantage.[47]

As confused as Newman seemed to be about the Catholic-Irish issue, so was he in other areas of his life during those years before his first trip to Italy. In matters of Christian Tradition, he had been enriched by his friends as they discussed apostolic succession or the role of Mary or the validity of the Roman Church. Yet, at the same time Newman would report that while Froude was "smitten with the love of the Theocratic Church; he went abroad and was shocked by the degeneracy which he thought he saw in the Catholics of Italy."[48] Despite getting such negative reports about the Italian people, Newman was still enjoying Italian music and entertainment. With Froude and a group of friends—"went all (but R.W.) to the Fantoccini (*They were very good and amusing—and altogether correct. Some undergraduate said 'There is that Methodist, Newman, here'.*)"[49]

Further, it would ultimately be Richard Hurrell Froude who would initiate John Henry Newman's first trip to Italy. During this trip, Newman would see the Italians as a whole and as individuals, and he would have an opportunity to relate to them as embodiments of Christian Tradition rather than as musicians, brigands, or Catholic degenerates. These Italians would be examples of compassionate believers who belonged to a Church that acknowledged oral Tradition, the holiness of the Blessed Mother, and the Communion of the Saints, when in the Anglican Church at that time, Scripture was the first and last court of appeal, the one and infallible source of faith; any authority attributed to Tradition beyond that of Scripture— which was the decisive point—would be an immediate breach of the Anglican system.[50]

Of course, this is not to say that Newman and his contemporaries would not find faults within the Italian society, especially

[47] Newman, "To Harriett Newman," *Letters and Diaries*, 2:132.
[48] *Apologia*, 42.
[49] Newman, "To Harriett Newman," *Letters and Diaries*, 2:319.
[50] See Biemer, *Newman on Tradition*, 24.

as they perceived the Italians' supposed ability to disjoin religion from morality. As has already been noted, Froude was shocked by the degeneracy he saw in the Italian Catholics. But, notwithstanding these real or imagined excesses on the part of the Italians, John Henry Newman did learn from them. He learned elements of Catholic Tradition that "enabled the convert to share with the cradle Catholic—especially if he were in the tradition of Philip Neri or von Hugel—a broad and deep humanism which accepts the Church as it is—warts and all. Entry into it, however, is both privilege and danger. Von Hugel, for example, often speaks of the Church as his hair shirt or purgatory, because conflict is inevitable in that which, by its perpetual growth, refuses to be confined to one modality. Yet, he concludes, 'What is a religion worth which costs you nothing?'"[51]

[51] John Coulson, *Newman and the Common Tradition* (Oxford: Clarendon Press, 1970), 178.

II

NEWMAN'S FIRST GLIMPSE OF ITALIAN RELIGIOUS TRADITION

The Prelude to Newman's First Trip to Italy

Thus, there can be no doubt that the elements the young Mr. Newman did admire about the Italians were their talents in composing and performing musical pieces. In fact, when in 1821 he achieved one of his greatest ambitions and composed "'a piece of music for instruments,'" he quickly wrote to his father about this success. "'I am glad to be able to inform you . . . that Signor Giovanni Enrico Neandri, has finished his first composition. The melody is light and airy, and is well supported by the harmony.'" [1]

When he wanted to be recognized for his musical abilities, Newman was proud to give himself the Italian name of Giovanni Neandri. Newman and his friends were enthralled with Italian music, and this feeling did not diminish as they grew older. As the 1820s gradually faded into the 30s, they were still talking and writing to each other about any exposure that they might have had to an Italian musician. Joseph Blanco White wrote to Newman in August of 1831—"I have heard Paganini. It is impossible to say too much either of his wonderful powers or of his sublime feeling. Imagine de Periot possessing six hands, and playing three fiddles; and yet Paganini would beat him. He does not perform one single difficulty which is not productive of the most perfect beauty." [2]

During this same time period, a dichotomy seems to have developed in Newman's mind. He knew that he loved the Italian music and especially their church music, but now he was

---

[1] J. Lewis May, *Cardinal Newman* (Westminster, Md.: The Newman Press, 1951), 36.
[2] Joseph Blanco White, 18 August 1831, in *Letters and Diaries*, 2:351.

wondering why his religion had become separated from their traditional Catholic Church. In one of his sermons of 1829, he began to address openly the problem of the Anglican broken unity:

> You know time was when there was but one vast body of Christians, called the Church, throughout the world. It was found in every country where the name of Christ was named: it was everywhere governed in the same way by bishops; it was everywhere descended from the Apostles through the line of those bishops; and it was everywhere in perfect peace and unity together, branch with branch, all over the world. . . . But now all this beauty . . . is defaced. That vast Catholic body, "the Holy Church throughout the world," is broken into many fragments by the power of the Devil; just as some huge barrier cliff which once boldly fronted the sea is at length cleft, parted, overthrown by the waves. Some portions of it are altogether gone, and those that remain are separated from each other. We are the English Catholics; abroad are the Roman Catholics, some of whom are among ourselves; else where are the Greek Catholics, and so on. And thus we stand in this day of rebuke and blasphemy—clinging to our portion of the Ancient Rock which the waters are raging round and would fain overflow.[3]

With an escalation of these feelings of alienation from the traditional Catholic Church, John Henry Newman was finding a new appreciation for the role of friends in his life. While at this point his friends were mainly "English Catholics" [i.e., "Anglicans"], he would one day forge lasting relationships with those "abroad who [were] Roman Catholics." As he said in the *Apologia*, "My habitual feeling then and since has been, that it was not I who sought friends, but friends who sought me. Never man had kinder or more indulgent friends than I have had; but I expressed my own feeling as to the mode in which I gained them, in this very year 1829, in the course of a copy of verses. Speaking of my blessings, I said, 'Blessings of friends, which to

[3] John Henry Newman, *Parochial and Plain Sermons*, vol. 2 (New York: Longmans, Green & Co., 1907), 191–192.

my door *unasked, unhoped,* have come.' They have come, they
have gone; they came to my great joy, they went to my great
grief. He who gave took away. . . ." [4]

Thus, in addition to his love of God and family, Newman
was most fond of his friends, and they often shared a common
appreciation of music. Just as he gave himself an Italian name
when he composed his first piece of music, so did Newman
often use Italian or Latin words (such as *carissime* or *dulcissime*)
when he addressed a letter to an especially dear friend. Perhaps he felt that the Italian (or Latin) language with its beauty
and rhythm would better convey his emotions than did his
native tongue. These details indicate that, even before he met
and became friends with individual Italians, Newman did hold
in esteem certain elements of Italian culture, and these "personal details, trivial though they seem, are illuminating, often
more illuminating than many pages of print; they convey to
the mind much that could never be adequately drawn out in
words." [5]

During these years, friendships were especially important to
Newman because changes were taking place in the tutorial
system at Oriel College, and Newman needed the support of his
friends to oppose some of these changes. "The appointment of
Froude and Wilberforce as tutors in 1828 meant that Newman
was no longer alone in his views As the new colleagues were
both 'disciples' of Keble, they were 'in practical agreement'
with Newman 'as to the nature of the office of College Tutor.'" [6] However, even with the support of his friends, Newman
realized that he would have to compromise more than he could
ethically agree to, and the "upshot of the whole affair, whereby
Newman, Froude, and Wilberforce were to 'die off gradually
without existing pupils,' was to Newman 'personally . . . a
delightful arrangement,' however bad he might think it for
the college, 'it will materially lessen my labours, and at length

[4] *Apologia,* 34.
[5] Henry Tristam, *Newman and His Friends* (London: John Lane, The Bodley Head, 1933), 26.
[6] Ian Ker, *John Henry Newman: A Biography* (Oxford University Press, 1988), 38.

reduce them within bearable limits.' More important, freedom from teaching duties meant that 'The Fathers arise up again full before me.'"[7] And, of course, this new-found lessening of responsibilities would ultimately give Newman the time and the freedom to make his first journey to the Continent and, most especially, to Italy.

Since the Provost gave him no new pupils, Newman found that each year the number of those that remained diminished, and his patristic reading grew more systematic. Probably the greatest benefit of Newman's increased study of the Fathers was that he was beginning to be more and more receptive to an appreciation of the Roman Catholic traditions, for the Church Fathers deepened his opposition to liberalism. However, the element of intolerance which was now visible in him had no affinity to the narrowness of his Calvinistic and Evangelical days. "Though he waged war on intellectualism, there was no return to a merely emotional religion. The vision of the Church Catholic grew ever more distinct. It embodied in its theology the results of the labours of the great thinkers of patristic times and their successors. That theology was a precious intellectual legacy, but it was also a standing protest against mere intellectualism. The sacred traditions inherited from the past were the basis of Christian theology and a touchstone of the truth of its more recent speculations."[8] As he was beginning to look away from intellectualism, Newman was now beginning to look towards the traditions of the Catholic Church.

In addition, Newman embarked upon a new endeavor which would further contribute towards his Catholic development.

> About 1830 a proposal was made to me by Mr. Hugh Rose, who with Mr. Lyall (afterwards Dean of Canterbury) was providing writers for a Theological Library, to furnish them with a History of the Principal Councils. I accepted it, and at once set to work on the Council of Nicaea. It was to launch myself on an ocean with currents innumerable; and I was

[7] Ibid., 41.
[8] Wilfred Ward, *The Life of John Henry Cardinal Newman* (London: Longmans, Green, and Co., 1912), 46.

drifted back first to the ante-Nicene history, and then to the Church of Alexandria. The work at last appeared under the title of *The Arians of the Fourth Century*, and of its 422 pages 117 consisted of introductory matter, and the Council of Nicaea did not appear till the 254th, and then occupied at most twenty pages.[9]

Newman probably sensed the importance of this work in his own life considering his ambivalent feelings about the lack of Tradition in the Church of England. He wrote about his excitement to Froude in August of 1831—"I have nothing to say, except that my work opens a grand and most interesting field to me—but how I shall ever be able to make one assertion, much less write one page I cannot tell—any one pure categorical, would need an age of reading and research—I shall confine myself to hypotheticals. Your 'if' [*sic*] is a great philosopher as well as peacemaker."[10]

As Wilfred Ward explained Newman's affinity for working on a book about the Arians:

> The subject was congenial to Newman for one reason especially. It was chiefly the state of the Church in the fourth century which enabled him to think of the Established Church of England as a part of the Church Catholic. He could not deny that the English Sees were in 1830 filled by Protestant bishops. But then so were multitudes of Catholic Sees in A.D. 360 filled by Arian bishops. He and his friends were in the position of faithful Catholics in those days, who kept the Faith in spite of their bishops. He could only hope that an Athanasius or a Basil would arise in England. Perhaps there was some subconscious presage that he himself might be destined to take the place of those great champions of truth in the nineteenth century. But with this historical parallel to give him confidence in his position, he considered in the course of his history the deeper problems of Christian faith and the analogy in the fourth century to his own campaign against liberalism and intellectualism.[11]

---

[9] *Apologia*, 43.
[10] Newman, "To Richard Hurrell Froude," *Letters and Diaries*, 2:348.
[11] Wilfred Ward, *Life of . . . Newman*, 47.

Thus, Newman saw himself and his friends as becoming cognizant of the Church as the Tradition-bearing body rather then just as the teacher of Scripture. "Scripture, says Newman, is not 'sufficient for the purposes of Christian fellowship.' It is Tradition, as proposed by the teaching Church in its role as expounder of Scripture, which gives the final word to preserving the faith of the community." [12] According to Newman:

> Scripture being unsystematic, and the faith which it propounds being scattered through its documents, and understood only when they are viewed as a whole, the Creeds aim at concentrating its general spirit, so as to give security to the Church, as far as may be, that its members take that definite view of that faith which alone is the true one. . . . If the Church be the pillar and ground of the truth, bound to contend for the preservation of the truth once delivered to it; if we are unanswerable as ministers of Christ for the formation of one, and one only, character in the heart of man; and if Scriptures are given us, as means indeed towards that end, but inadequate to the office of interpreting themselves, except to such as live under the same Divine Influence which inspired them, and which is expressly sent down upon us that we may interpret them—then, it is evidently our duty piously and cautiously to collect the sense of Scripture, and solemnly to promulgate it in such a form as is best suited, as far as it goes, to exclude the pride and unbelief of the world. [13]

From his writings in the *Arians*, it can be seen that Newman had already taken for granted the existence of Tradition in the Church of the Fathers. "His only question was how it could be preserved from corruption in the course of time. And his final answer was that he found that Tradition was given a fixed and unaltered expression in the Creeds of the Church. . . . Another doctrine of Newman's found in its initial stages in the *Arians*, was to become of far-reaching importance. This was the function of lay-people in the general process of Tradition." [14]

[12] Lease, *Witness to the Faith*, 20.

[13] John Henry Cardinal Newman, *The Arians of the Fourth Century* (Westminster, Md.: Christian Classics, 1968), 147–148.

[14] Biemer, *Newman on Tradition*, 38–39.

The Arians of the Fourth Century was finished in June of 1832, but its writing had taken a toll on Newman—"my health had suffered from the labour involved in the composition of my Volume." [15] Newman was about to embark upon another adventure—his first trip to the European continent and, most especially, to Italy. During this maiden voyage, Newman would have an opportunity to observe, first-hand, how Church Tradition was promulgated in Italy and what role the laity played in transmitting such Tradition.

The Voyage to the Mediterranean with the Froudes

In the following letter, Newman was invited to Italy by his friend Richard Froude:

FROM RICHARD HURRELL FROUDE

Sept. 9. 1832

Dulcissime N

I have had my ups and downs since I saw you, and the latter in close proximity to the former. . . . You will be glad to hear that I have made up my mind to spend the winter in the Mediterranean; my Father is going with me the end of November—and we shall see Scicily [*sic*] and the South of Italy—we are both very anxious that you should come with us—I think it would set you up—and you might easily make arrangements—cutting the Deanship for this year—my Father will be the best person in the world for finding out what is worth seeing. Can you come down here and talk the scheme over—you shall not have so expansive a journey again. [16]

With these few words from his most Catholic of friends, John Henry Newman would begin a lifelong odyssey with Italy and the Italian people. He was sorely tempted by Froude's offer, and he did not take much time to respond:

---

[15] *Apologia*, 47.
[16] Richard Hurrell Froude, "Dulcissime N," 9 September 1832, in *Letters and Diaries*, 3:92.

September 13. 1832

My dear F

Your letter, which I received yesterday, was very welcome. . . . I am much tempted by your proposal for several
reasons. . . . Then what a name the Mediterranean is! and
the time of year, for I think summer would be too hot for me;
and the opportunity of getting there without touching Gallic
earth, (for I suppose you go by water) which is an abomina-
tion. . . . And if I *ever* am to travel, is not this the time that I
am most at liberty for it?. . . . and I feel the need of it; I am
suspicious of becoming narrow-minded, and at least I wish
to experience the feeling and the trial of expansiveness of
views, if it were but to be able to *say* I had, and to know how
to meet it in the case of others. . . .[17]

Newman seemed excited about the prospect of going abroad
and, most specifically, to the Mediterranean countries. Interestingly, he wanted no part of even touching upon French soil but
made no mention of any overt distaste for Italy. In fact, he was
anxious to broaden his viewpoints, and Italy was the destination
that he talked about the most. When he wrote to his pupil
Frederic Rogers in October, he said, "We intend to go, by the
beginning of December, straight to Sicily, Italy, or any where
else we please. . . . If you can give any introductions to persons
at Malta, in Sicily, Naples, Rome or Corfu, nay or Alexandria,
you may do so. . . ."[18]

On Sunday, 2 December 1832, John Henry Newman delivered the last university sermon that he was to preach until 1839.
About one o'clock on the following Saturday, he set sail with the
Froudes from Falmouth, England, on board the packet *Hermes*.
"Three days later he penned the first of the many descriptive
letters he was to send home."[19] These letters would be Newman's own testimony of his growing fascination with the country of Italy and its people—a fascination that would be ignited
during this first trip and would grow in intensity until the day of

---

[17] Newman, "To Richard Hurrell Froude," in *Letters and Diaries*, 3:93.
[18] Newman, "To Frederic Rogers," in *Letters and Diaries*, 3:102.
[19] Ian Ker, *John Henry Newman*, 55.

his death. Further, as he and his companions were traveling down past Portugal, into Gibraltar, then Malta and Greece, Newman kept reflecting upon how his Church had become separated from the Church that had originated in those lands. He seemed to be searching for some aspects of Christian Tradition that were lacking in his Anglican Church.

Early in the voyage, Newman expressed this longing in a poem that he included in a letter to his sister Jemima:

> *Poor wanderers, you are sore perplexed*
> *To find that path which Christ has blest,*
> *Tracked by His saintly throng:*
> *Each claims to trust his own weak will,*
> *Blind idol; so ye languish still*
> *All wranglers, and all wrong.*
>
> *He saw of old, and felt your need,*
> *Granting you prophets of His creed,*
> *The throes of fear to swage;*
> *They stored the rich bequest he made,*
> *And sacred hands have safe conveyed*
> *The charge from age to age.*
>
> *Wanderers, come home! When erring most,*
> *The Church aye kept the faith, nor lost*
> *One grain of holy truth,*
> *She ne'er has erred as those you trust,*
> *And soon she shall shake off her dust,*
> *And REIGN as in her youth.*[20]

Newman was now at a distance from his homeland and from the Church of England, and this poem clearly reflects an incipient ambiguity about the road that his Church had taken. Interestingly, he spoke of the search for the "path of Christ" and "the sacred hands" which conveyed the Tradition of Christianity

---

[20] Newman, "My Dear Jemima," in *Letters and Diaries*, 3:139.

"from age to age." But, who was "all wrong," and was it the Anglican Church or the Catholic Church which had kept the Faith but needed to "shake off her dust"? Whatever Newman was thinking as he wrote these lines will never truly be known, but he will have more definite impressions of the Catholic Church after his sojourn in Italy, and his visit will greatly increase his dualism towards Catholicism and how the Italians conveyed the traditions of their religion.

The Froudes and Newman were the only passengers on the *Hermes,* which took them to Gibraltar, Cadiz, Algiers, Zante, Patras, Corfu, and then as far as Malta. They were held up for several weeks in the Lazaretto at Malta because of quarantine restrictions for the cholera epidemic. However, Newman used this time well, for "Thursday 24 January, took my first Italian lesson with Mr Lombardo," and "Saturday 26 January, 3rd and 4th Italian lessons." [21] Already Newman knew that he wanted to learn Italian rather than any other European language.

On February 7, after having completed fifteen Italian lessons in Malta, Newman left with the Froudes on a steamer bound for Naples. En route, they spent five nights in Sicily, stopping at Messina, Palermo, and Egesta. Newman felt an immediate love for the scenery and history of Sicily, if not for the people. ". . . Sicily; which (little as I have seen of it) has filled me with inexpressible rapture, and to which (in spite of dirt and other inconveniences) I feel drawn as by a loadstone. . . .The chief sight being the ruins of Egesta (Segesta) with its temple!—oh wonderful sight and full of the most strange pleasure, from the wonderful position of the town, its awful desolateness, the strange beauty of the scenery, rich even in winter, and its historical recollections, and, last not least, the misery of the population, the depth of squalidness and brutality, by which it is surrounded." [22]

This rapture for Sicily would be the starting point for Newman's lifelong fascination with Italy and the Italians. Sicily was

[21] Notes in *Letters and Diaries,* 3:203.
[22] Newman "To Harriet Newman," in *Letters and Diaries,* 3:211.

the site of so much history and, also, was the link between the classical world and the Christian world. In Sicily one found the beginnings of all recorded Tradition:

> The history of which, beginning with the highest antiquity, was united with the histories of both Greece and Rome, which had never been an unknown recorded place, and was the theme of every poet and every historian of antiquity, and which had remains in it more ancient and perfect than those of any country. . . . The past and the present! What a contrast from the time when the two hills were full of life. I began to understand what Scripture means by speaking so much of cities set upon hills—what a noble but ungodly sight it must have been, like Satan himself, the mockery and imitation of true greatness, when this place was in its glory. And then its historical associations—to say nothing of Virgil's fictions, here it was that Nicias came—this was the ally of Athens. What a strange wild place! how did people ever take it into their heads to settle here![23]

From the middle of February until the beginning of March 1833, Newman and his companions were in Naples, a city that did not much impress John Newman. "There was nothing to offend me, however, more than the whole city itself—which does offend me very much—It is a frivolous dissipated place—this is Carnival-time and all sorts of silly public Saturnalia between King and people are going on and religion is turned into a mere medium of gaiety and worldly festivity, as in the case of the Israelites—and the sooner we are out of so bad a place, the better."[24]

During those days both in Sicily and in Naples, Newman was evaluating what he perceived to be the state of the Catholic Church. With an ostensibly overt condemnation came a hint of ambivalence:

> The state of the Church is deplorable. It seems as if Satan were let out of prison to range the whole earth again. As far as our little experience goes, every thing seems to confirm

---

[23] Newman, "To Jemima Newman," in *Letters and Diaries*, 3:215–220.
[24] Ibid., 3:216.

the notion received among ourselves of the infidelity and profligacy of the priesthood—while the Church on the other hand is stripped of its temporalities and reduced to great distress. . . . I heard also . . . that . . . the Sicilian Church was expected to support the poor—that they compounded for this by giving a certain sum to Government *instead*, which sum is now appropriated to the payment of *government pensions*! . . . At Naples, the poverty of the Church is deplorable. . . . Thus, as far as we have seen, these countries have all the evil of Protestantism without its advantages, i.e. of Anglican Protestantism for nothing can excuse schism. . . . But here also they have infidelity and profaneness—as if the whole world (Western) were tending towards some dreadful crisis. I begin to hope that England is after all to be the "Land of Saints" in this dark hour, and her Church the salt of the earth. . . . Doubtless there are God's saints here and perhaps brighter than with us. We heard of one man (at Messina, I think) who while bearing his witness against the profligacy of the priesthood, rigidly attends Mass—and on being asked why, said the Altar was above the priest, and that God could bless His own ordinance in spite of base instruments.[25]

Newman could deplore what he saw as a corrupt church, but he felt admiration for those individuals who kept alive the beauty and the Christian Tradition of the Church Fathers and the saints.

Early in March, John Henry Newman arrived for the very first time in Rome, a place that would be the scene of many momentous events in his life. One of Newman's biographers, Maisie Ward, described his conflicting feelings: "From Rome a burst of correspondence with all his friends conveys much of Newman's strange state of mind: passionate admiration fights with lifelong suspicion." [26]

Newman's confusion was apparent also in a letter to his friend, Frederic Rogers, in which he discussed his impressions of Rome. "Of course, I have seen very little of it; but the effect of every part is so vast and overpowering—there is such an air of

---

[25] Newman, "To Mrs Newman," in *Letters and Diaries*, 3:224–225.
[26] Maisie Ward, *Young Mr. Newman* (New York: Sheed & Ward, 1948), 201.

greatness and repose cast over the whole, and independent of what one knows from history, there are such traces of long sorrow and humiliation, suffering, punishment and decay, that one has a mixture of feelings, partly such as those with which one would approach a corpse, and partly those which would be excited by the sight of the spirit which had left it. . . . No words can describe [the churches]. They could not have been in any place but Rome, which has turned the materials and the buildings of the Empire to the purposes of religion." [27]

Maisie Ward also made mention of Newman's confusion between a love of the city of Rome and a hatred for the religion of Rome:

> While most of the letters dwell on the glory of the city and condemn the existing Church, one to Samuel Richards, written a few days later from Naples, works out in some detail a curious theory. Rome is Babylon, is accursed, but this means the city of Rome, not necessarily its Church. St. Gregory had recognized this when he ordered the destruction of the monuments of pagan Rome. A Roman tradition emphasized that no human power could destroy the city. St. Gregory had believed it "reserved for future superhuman judgments." The temporal power of the Papacy had in some way involved the great Apostasy. By an old Irish prophecy the line of Popes was now within nine or ten of its close—at the end of the list we read, "Then shall she that sitteth upon the seven hills be destroyed when the Lord shall come to judge the earth." [28]

Newman reinforced this sentiment in a letter to John Frederic Christie:

> Well then, again after this, you have to view Rome as a place of religion—and here what mingled feelings come upon one. You are in the place of martyrdom and burial of Apostles and saints—you have about you the buildings and sights they saw—and you are in the city to which England owes the blessing of the gospel—But then on the other hand the

[27] Newman, "To Frederic Rogers," in *Letters and Diaries*, 3:234–235.
[28] Maisie Ward, *Young Mr. Newman*, 202.

superstitions;—or rather, what is far worse, the solemn reception of them as an essential part of Christianity—but then again the extreme beauty and costliness of the Churches—and then on the contrary the knowledge that the most famous was built (in part) by the sale of indulgences—Really this is a cruel place.—There is more and more to be seen and thought of, daily—it is a mine of all sorts of excellences, but the very highest.[29]

Just before leaving Rome, Newman revisited Santa Maria in Cosmedin, and his thoughts turned to Pope Dionysius, who founded it, and to St. Augustine of Canterbury, who studied there. As Louis Bouyer has said, "We cannot help wondering how amazed he would have been—he who always thought so much of providential signs and premonitions—could it have been revealed to him, in a momentary vision of things to come, that one day, in the still distant future, he would be Cardinal titular of the neighbouring church of San Giorgio in Velabro. He mounts the Janicular [*sic*] once more and pays a farewell visit to the tomb of St Peter." [30]

Thus, Newman would hate to leave the beautiful city of Rome, but, at this point in his life, he felt no compunction about leaving the Italian people themselves. Revolting filth, beggars pushing their way everywhere, sloth, dishonesty—all these things shocked him as they were calculated to shock any average Anglo-Saxon tourist. He was left with an idea of a Christianity devitalized within itself by an excessive external and too worldly exuberance.[31] Newman thought that the people of Italy, indeed the peoples of most of southern Europe, had taken the Christian Tradition that had been handed down from the Church of the Apostles and corrupted its purity with needless superstition and excessiveness. But, for now, Newman had had his first Roman experience, and the passage of time and the influence of several Italian friends would some day help him to realize that the Church of Rome could still be the Church of the Apostles.

---

[29] Newman, "To John Frederic Christie," in *Letters and Diaries*, 3:241.

[30] Bouyer, *Newman*, 137.

[31] See ibid., 135–137.

The Illness in Sicily

While years would pass before Newman could accept the Church of Rome as his own, his experience in Sicily gave him a great opportunity to witness, firsthand, the kindliness and humanity of individual Italians and to begin to understand the Catholic concept of the role of Providence in one's life. He had had his first taste of Sicily with the Froudes in February, 1833. From that moment on, he would forever be enamored of those first visions of that exotic and isolated island. In fact, many years later when he was writing *Callista*, he once again referred to Sicily. Describing the African city of Sicca Veneria—"At the extreme back, towards the north, which could not be seen from the point of view where we last stationed ourselves, there was a sheer descent of rock, bestowing on the city, when it was seen at a distance on the Mediterranean side, the same bold and striking appearance which attaches to Castro Giovanni, the ancient Enna, in the heart of Sicily." [32]

This fascination with Sicily was surprising, and Newman must have been totally smitten, because all during his Mediterranean tour he had professed an intense longing for England. The thought of England recurred often in the verses written for the *Lyra Apostolica*, and in several of his letters he wrote that he was homesick. Further, he was constantly getting letters from home that described the disturbing news of the political situation in England concerning the Irish Church Reform Bill. "With all this going on back home and him far away, unable to take any part in helping to prevent what he was sure would be further disasters, Newman felt more than ever a stranger in these foreign lands. When Cardinal Wiseman expressed the wish that he and the Froudes might return for a second visit to Rome, his only reply was: 'We have a work to do in England.' The odd thing is that, when the Froudes shortly afterward decided to cancel the rest of their tour and return home, Newman

[32] John Henry Newman, *Callista: A Sketch of the Third Century* (New York: Sheed & Ward, 1941), 10.

parted company with them. The Froudes went back to England; Newman went off in the opposite direction, to Sicily." [33]

This second trip to Sicily would be remembered by Newman as one of the most important moments in his life—both as an opportunity to meet sincere Italian people and as an example of the role of Providence in his life. The trip was so significant that Newman was compelled to write about it in August of 1834: "I have wished for some time to write in this book an account of my illness in Sicily (in May 1833); for the remembrance is pleasant and profitable." [34]

Because of Newman's emphasis upon its importance, this Sicilian sojourn is well documented and quite interesting:

> He parted company with the Froudes on April 9, [they] setting out to Civita Vecchia en route to France and home, and he to Naples with Sicily as his objective. There he made his preparations for the journey, his equipment consisting of a "set of cooking utensils and tea service—curry powder, spice, pepper, salt, sugar, tea, and ham;". . . He also engaged a servant to accompany him, Gennaro by name, a "trustyman". . . . After a delay of nine days he secured a passage in a sailing vessel. . . and on Friday, April 19, he left Naples. . . . The next day, Saturday, April 20, the ship lay becalmed off Stromboli, but it reached Messina on Sunday, April 21, between 6 and 7 a.m. [35]

The following day, Newman and his "cavalcade consisting of servant, muleteer, and mules," set off by foot southwards from Messina. They reached Taormina, where the view from the ancient theater was "a nearer approach to seeing Eden, than anything" he "had conceived possible." This magnificent scenery had a profound spiritual effect upon him: "I felt for the first time in my life with my eyes open that I must be better and more religious, if I lived there." They went on to the foot of Mt. Etna, but because of the snow upon it, Newman did not attempt

---

[33] Sheridan, *Newman on Justification*, 209–210.

[34] *John Henry Newman: Autobiographical Writings*, ed. Henry Tristram (New York: Sheed & Ward, 1957), 121. (Hereafter: *Autobiographical Writings*.)

[35] Quoted in *Autobiographical Writings*, 111.

to climb it.[36] As never before, Newman was seeing the possibility of living a holier life as a result of being personal witness to the awesomeness of God's work.

Despite the beautiful landscape, Newman was experiencing a strained leg and his feet were covered in blisters from walking. He and his group spent the night in Catania where they cleaned up and rested before taking the boat to Syracuse. Because of heavy rain, they were blown off course and had to spend the night in a cove only a few miles from Syracuse. They returned to Catania, rested, and then set out by foot for Leonforte. Newman was already feeling under the weather with feverish symptoms. As he rested in bed there, "he felt he was being punished for self-will (his last sermon before leaving Oxford had been on the sin of willfulness) in leaving the Froudes and coming on his own. . . . Still, nobody had actually advised him against coming to Sicily, and he 'kept saying' to himself 'I have not sinned against the light.' "[37] Somehow Sicily had become a light or represented the light of God to which he was irresistibly drawn.

Refusing to accept the fact that he was seriously ill, Newman insisted, in his somewhat delirious state, to set out again on his tour of Sicily. But they had gone only a short distance when he began to feel suffocated in his throat, and they had to rest in a hut. Towards evening he was sufficiently recovered to be put on a mule, and he was then taken to the nearby town of Castro Giovanni where the doctor attempted to bleed him. "It seemed he had fallen victim to an epidemic of gastric or typhoid fever, from which numbers of people were dying, and which was often accompanied by cholera."[38]

Interestingly enough, in addition to the spiritual significances of this sickness, people have been fascinated by its medical aspects. One physician, Dr. Howard Slavin, has diagnosed the illness: "Most of Newman's physical sufferings during the

---

[36] Ian Ker, *John Henry Newman*, 75.
[36] Ibid., 76.
[38] Ibid., 77.

earlier acute stages of his illness are common enough in typhoid. They include aching of the legs, weakness. . . . Even an
oppressive weight of the bedclothes is by no means rare in the
personal observations of the author." [39]

In those days, typhoid was a most critical illness, and there
was a distinct possibility that Newman might have succumbed
to the disease. However, finally the fever reached its peak on
May 13, and within a few days, Newman started to make a
recovery. After about a week, he took his first walk outside,
and, at last, on Saturday, May 25, they left Castro Giovanni
bound for Palermo on an orange-boat that would take him to
Marseilles. On this final leg of his trip through Sicily, "Newman
was overwhelmed by the beauty of the countryside—'Spring in
its greatest luxuriance.' . . . He had returned to Sicily for two
reasons: first, to see its antiquities, which he had failed to do,
and second, to see the countryside, about which he could 'only
say that I did not know before nature could be so beautiful'—it
was indeed 'like the garden of Eden' and surpassed all his
expectations." [40]

In addition to concluding that Sicily had the most beautiful
landscape in the world, Newman was forever changed and
inspired by his sojourn there. He had an awakening about the
Italian people whom he had previously considered only from
afar and very stereotypically. He now had had the opportunity
to see them as good and kind and worthy of his respect and his
friendship. He would never forget his loyal travel companion,
Gennaro, upon whom he was totally dependent during his
illness. This Italian man would remain etched in his mind and
heart as no other—"I left Gennaro at Palermo; he was to go
back to Naples to his wife and family. . . . He was humanly
speaking the preserver of my life, I think. What I should have
done without him, I cannot think. He nursed me as a child. An
English servant never could do what he did." [41]

[39] Howard B. Slavin, M.D., "Newman's Illness in Sicily: A Review and an Interpretation," *Dublin Review* 238 (1964): 52.
[40] Ian Ker, *John Henry Newman*, 78–79.
[41] Newman, in *Autobiographical Writings*, 138.

This important acknowledgment by Newman that an Italian could be more caring and receptive to helping others than even one from his own country was further enforced by other people whom he had encountered. Throughout the journey, "The natives they met were polite and helpful, although obviously very poor, and Newman liked what he saw of them—'dirt, but simplicity and contentment.'"[42] And there were others. Newman had only good things to say about the owner of the inn where he stayed in Castro Giovanni:

> Providentially, as he found out by experience, he had fallen into good hands. His host, whose name was Luigi Vestivo, and those about him, spent themselves to the utmost on behalf of the stranger whom chance had placed under their care. Before Newman left for Palermo some weeks later, Vestivo asked him for some record of the time of his involuntary sojourn among them, and he wrote the following note in a book or on a sheet of paper: *"Joannes Henricus Newman, Anglus, in his aedibus libentissimo hospitio exceptus est, curatus, sanatus. Mens. Maii 24, 1833."* On his return to England, he also sent him, in response to his request, a Bible, presumably in the Authorized Version, accompanied by a letter. . . . What impressed Newman deeply, apart from their kindness, was the absolute honesty of his host and of all who looked after him.[43]

Even the Italian doctor who attended him during his illness was to make a lifelong impression upon the Englishman:

> Newman had picked up a certain smattering of Italian during his travels, but with the oncoming of his illness, as he tells us, his limited knowledge of the language vanished completely from his mind. Since the doctor who attended him did not command even a smattering of English, it became a problem how they could make contact with each other. They hit upon a way out of the *impasse* by having recourse to Latin, which Newman had not forgotten, and of which the doctor still retained his early memories, relying, however, not on the spoken, but on the written word, as the channel of communication. The paper on which they jotted down their

---

[42] Ian Ker, *John Henry Newman*, 76.
[43] Tristram, in *Autobiographical Writings*, 113–114.

questions and answers, Newman brought back with him to England, and preserved to the end of his life.[44]

Thus, the illness in Sicily gave Newman an opportunity to observe the unique capacity within the Italian people to give selflessly of themselves to others, even to a complete stranger of another nationality. For the first time in his life, John Henry Newman witnessed an entire society of Roman Catholics, became friends with some of them, and could observe how their religious traditions were inherent in all aspects of their lives.

On the contrary, as an Anglican child growing up in nineteenth-century England, Newman had never really come into contact with Catholics, for "social life among the Catholic aristocracy in England had been so closely circumscribed under the penal laws, and the old families had intermarried so many times, that they lived in a world of their own, which those outside it often misjudged."[45] Newman, in his famous sermon titled "Second Spring," recorded his youthful impressions of being apart from the Catholics in his country—"Here a set of poor Irishmen, coming and going at harvest time, or a colony of them lodged in a miserable quarter of the vast metropolis. There, perhaps an elderly person, seen walking in the streets, grave and solitary, and strange, though noble in bearing, and said to be of good family, and a 'Roman Catholic.' An old-fashioned house of gloomy appearance . . . and the report attaching to it that 'Roman Catholics' lived there; but who they were, or what they did, or what was meant by calling them Roman Catholics, no one could tell—though it had an unpleasant sound, and told of form and superstition."[46]

The status of Catholics in England did not greatly improve as Newman matured, and he had little understanding of their religious practices. For the most part, Catholic families had "a long tradition of being obliged to say their prayers almost in secret in

[44] Ibid., 114.

[45] Denis Gwynn, *Father Dominic Barberi* (Buffalo, N.Y.: Desmond & Stapleton, 1948), 47.

[46] Newman "The Second Spring," in *Sermons Preached on Various Occasions* (London: Longmans, Green, and Co., 1892), 171–172.

their own houses," and Bishop Wiseman noted that English Catholics were "just emerging from the catacombs." [47] Therefore, in Sicily, Newman was to be submerged for the first time into a society where almost everyone viewed Catholicism as the intrinsic defining structure of both the social and religious lives.

Even when Newman had been in main-land Italy, he did not make the acquaintance of native Italians as he would in Sicily. Rome had been filled with English visitors, and Newman spent most of his time with his fellow countrymen. When he discussed Rome and religion in his letters home, his comments were very superficial: "The Roman Clergy are said to be a decorous orderly body—and certainly most things are very different from Naples. . . . But there is (seemingly) timidity, indolence, and that secular spirit which creeps on established religion everywhere." [48] In Sicily, however, Newman saw peasants crowded into churches for early morning Masses, and he personally witnessed manifestations of their piety as they gently and kindly ministered to him in his grave illness.

In addition, Newman's perception of his sickness and its importance in his life was to open another stage in his religious development—an openness to the ways of God's Providence in determining the path of one's existence. How startling that this new revelation would come to Newman in Italy—the place where *la Provvidenza di Dio* [the Providence of God] is a significant element of Italian religious tradition. And, in the future, it would be the common bond of interest in the concept of *la Provvidenza* that would draw Newman to other Italians, including Alessandro Manzoni and Giovanni Perrone.

Divine Providence is "the plan by which God orders all things to their true end." [49] To Newman, God's plan was brought into sharp focus by his illness. "I seem to see, and I saw, a strange providence in it." [50] As Roderick Strange has described its significance:

[47] Gwynn, *Father Dominic Barberi*, 60.
[48] Newman, "My Dear Harriet," in *Letters and Diaries*, 3:232.
[49] "Providence of God," *Our Sunday Visitor Catholic Encyclopedia*, 825.
[50] Newman, *Autobiographical Writings*, 121.

To understand the working of Providence as Newman perceived it in the light of his Sicilian visit, it is essential to remember that there was no trace of his wrestling with God, his brooding on his failings, or his dark judgment of himself, until the illness struck. Here was the strange Providence, the cause of surprise and wonder. His perilous condition brought about a revelation of divine presence. His declining fortunes in Oxford, his resentment at the Provost, the general state of fatigue which had led him to join the Froudes for this holiday, may all have combined, even in him whose sense of God's presence was so vivid, to dull his awareness of that presence. The illness revived it.

It was a crisis whose effects were spiritual as well as physical. Suddenly he saw the obstacles which had troubled him since leaving the Froudes in Rome—presumably the delays and difficulties which had beset his return to the island—as signs of God fighting against him. He recognized the poor manner of his behavior over the tutorial dispute and the way his resentment of the Provost had, as he judged it, made his reception of the Eucharist unworthy. And in his very journey to Sicily he discovered a particular example of the general willfulness which, he concluded, marred his character. He indulged his own will too much. He seemed at least to resemble Saul who had "preferred his own way to that which God had determined." Here there was lacking that unreserved self-surrender and submission to the divine will which he had so urged upon others. Nevertheless, in spite of these hazards, his resistance to God and willfulness, he felt comforted even in the depths of his sickness. He was comforted, he told Wilberforce, because he had not gone against my advice which he had actually received and because he had not "sinned against the light." And then, he added, "I thought I would try to obey God's will as far as I could." What a strange providence indeed to have been so preserved from sin and then enlightened by grave illness.[51]

At last, having been saved from death and enlightened by God's will, John Henry Newman left Italy on 13 June 1833. Because of his experiences in that beautiful land, his life would never be the same. He had begun to know the Italian people, and he had an understanding of their willingness to put aside their own self-interests in their obedience to God and to His commandments. "All the feelings and sentiments of Newman that came forth from his illness find themselves expressed in his famous poem 'Lead, Kindly Light.' Therein is reflected a serene humility, a peaceful confidence, and an abandonment to God, all of which gives an assurance of spiritual progress and a hopeful end." [52] "Lead, Kindly Light," or "The Pillar of the Cloud" as Newman entitled it, would become one of the most famous of all English poems and would be memorized by future generations of English schoolchildren:

> *Lead, kindly light, amid the encircling gloom,*
> *Lead Thou me on!*
> *The night is dark, and I am far from home—*
> *Lead Thou me on!*
> *Keep Thou my feet; I do not ask to see*
> *The distant scene,—one step enough for me.*
>
> *I was not ever thus, nor prayed that Thou*
> *Shouldst lead me on.*
> *I loved to choose and see my path; but now,*
> *Lead Thou me on!*
> *I loved the garish day, and, spite of fears,*
> *Pride ruled my will: remember not past years!*
>
> *So long Thy power hath blessed me, sure it still*
> *Will lead me on,*
> *O'er moor and fen, o'er crag and torrent, till*
> *The night is gone;*
> *And with the morn those angel faces smile*
> *Which I have loved long since, and lost awhile.* [53]

[52] Jean Cardinal Honoré, *The Spiritual Journey of Newman* (New York: Alba House, 1992), 100.

[53] John Henry Newman, "The Pillar of the Cloud," in *Verses on Various Occasions* (London: Burns and Oates, 1883), 152–153.

III

AN INTRODUCTION TO CATHOLICISM

*Newman's Concept of Tradition
during the Oxford Movement*

There can be no doubt that there was a different and more trusting spirituality manifesting itself in John Henry Newman because of his experience in Sicily. In fact, he began to acknowledge openly the efficacy of God's Providence. Exactly a year later he would write: "Now it certainly is remarkable that a new and large sphere of action has opened upon me from the very moment I returned . . . and altogether my name, which was not known out of Oxford circles before I went abroad, is now known pretty generally. My sermons have sold very well. Now in all this there seems something remarkable and providential. O my God, keep me still from being the sport and victim of Satan. By Thy Mercies in Thy Son's Holy Table which I have this day partaken, be to me a Saviour." [1]

Newman's sermons were indeed doing well, and the major thrust of his outpourings "was the urgency of a spiritual revival in the dormant, unthinking, unfeeling Church of England, which should rather be inspired by a clear recognition of its direct succession from the apostolic Church. For its proponents, this affiliation implied a greater sympathy towards Rome and a greater ritualization of worship. In an academic community explicitly defined as a bastion of Anglican orthodoxy, this stance could not but prove profoundly divisive. The arguments propagated by Newman and his sympathizers were set forth in

---

[1] Hilda Graef, *God and Myself: The Spirituality of John Henry Newman* (New York: Hawthorn Books, 1968), 45–46.

tracts and thus their campaign became known as Tractarianism and later simply as 'the Oxford Movement.'" [2]

Many times throughout his future writings, Newman would attest that he was a changed man when he returned from Italy. And even though the circumstances of his existence were again the same, he had a new inspiration with which to confront the problems at home. As he said in the *Apologia*:

> I have not exaggerated the feelings with which I returned to England, and I have no desire to dress up the events which followed, so as to make them in keeping with the narrative which has gone before. I soon relapsed into the every-day life which I had hitherto led; in all things the same, except that a new object was given me. I had employed myself in my own rooms in reading and writing, and in the care of a Church, before I left England, and I returned to the same occupations when I was back again. And yet perhaps those first vehement feelings which carried me on, were necessary for the beginning of the Movement; and afterwards, when it was once begun, the special need of me was over. [3]

Also in the *Apologia*, Newman assigned the beginning of the Oxford Movement to Keble's sermon on "National Apostasy," preached in the University Pulpit on 14 July 1833. The sermon seemed to have made a great impression on Newman, and he asked for some copies of it. "For he had returned from Italy just a few days before he heard it, full of new vigour and the conviction that the Church of England was in a bad state and something must be done about it. Keble expressed exactly what Newman and also the other leaders of the Movement felt, hence he dated the beginning of the Movement from this sermon." [4]

Just as he had been so changed by the inspiration that he brought home from Italy, so did Newman feel that a new spirit needed to be instilled into the Church of England. As

[2] Richard Tames, *A Traveller's History of Oxford* (New York: Interlink Books, 2003), 170.

[3] *Apologia*, 51.

[4] Graef, *God and Myself*, 7.

Jean Honoré described the atmosphere to which Newman returned:

> In the 1830s, the drama for the Anglican Church was not so much that it was unaware of its own peril. It seemed to have lost a clear notion of its situation with regard to the State. Multiple interferences by the Crown against the Church were, everything considered, less dangerous than the feeling of security with which it tolerated such conduct. The audacity shown by the government in its interferences in religious affairs was only a symptom of the profound apathy which pervaded the Church, to the point of forgetting her own dignity. Her own interests were disregarded because she had lost all feeling of pride. Parliament voted the Reform Bill which suppressed ten Anglican bishoprics in Ireland. Backed by the servile silence and oftentimes the complacency of ecclesiastical dignitaries, the liberals, in total quietude, were able to press for more and more audacious projects which all tended to tighten more strictly the Church to the English Crown. Arnold, the best known of the liberal leaders, went so far as to declare: "In its present situation, can any human power save the Church?"[5]

Little did people, especially the liberals, realize that valiant attempts would be made to save the Church. There were several young men who were not apathetic about what they saw happening to their beloved institution, and they were ready to act. For John Henry Newman, the new work that he had envisioned in Sicily had begun. During the years 1834 and 1835, Newman "edited numerous tracts, some of them among the most incisive; he wrote letter upon letter, traveling throughout the countryside in order to bring tracts just off the presses to the vicarages. Throughout the entire course of these years, which were only a prelude to what was coming, one can feel a hardly contained enthusiasm and a juvenile fervor."[6]

At the same time, Newman was searching also for the spirituality that he had witnessed on his trip. In Italy he had seen a vibrant, living Catholic Church with traditions that had existed

---

[5] Honoré, *Spiritual Journey of Newman*, 103–104.
[6] Ibid., 106.

for centuries. As he lovingly recounted: "And my heart was touched also. Making an expedition on foot across some wild country in Sicily, at six in the morning, I came upon a small church; I heard voices, and I looked in. It was crowded, and the congregation was singing. Of course, it was the Mass, though I did not know it at the time."[7] Newman seemed to ache for this type of spirituality in his own country, and he started to look more and more upon the role of Tradition as a means to convey this enthusiasm from one generation to the next.

In addition, there were some specific elements that Newman saw in Catholic Tradition that he felt were missing in his own Church, and a good part of these years was spent in trying to justify the Anglican position or to understand further the Catholic one. To this end, in 1834 and 1835 Newman carried on a controversy by letters with a Parisian priest, the Abbé Jean Nicolas Jager. In the course of this correspondence, Newman described his concept of Tradition under three aspects: a Tradition which interprets Scripture, a Tradition independent of Scripture (which can be justified by Scripture, e.g., infant baptism), and a tradition concerned with discipline, ceremonies (customs), and historical facts. He felt that Catholic Tradition added a fourth aspect which considered Tradition *per se* the sufficient authority for the Church's considering a doctrine fundamental.[8] As Newman postulated this further condition to the Abbé:

> But in your letter to me, you were speaking not of the *terms of communion*, but of doctrines necessary to salvation. True— but it was you who began speaking of fundamentals, which to me mean *nothing else* than terms of communion. Drop the word fundamental and take the latter, and then see what I have said. I quote my words. Perhaps you will ask, Why do you Anglicans make such a difference between the written and the unwritten word? If the belief in the one is necessary to salvation so is belief in the other. We answer, first of all,

[7] *Apologia*, 61.
[8] See Günter Biemer, *Newman on Tradition* (New York: Herder and Herder, 1967), 43–44.

that on the very first face of the matter, it is clear that Scripture does absolutely declare belief in its doctrines necessary to salvation, but Tradition (i.e., Prophetical) does not say so of its own. . . . Scripture and Tradition, taken *per se*, come to us in a different aspect; the one with a demand upon our faith, the other not.[9]

With these questions and dialogues, Newman was attempting to understand the complexity of Tradition as a means of promulgating Christian doctrine. All of this thought culminated in one of his most significant works, *Lectures on the Prophetical Office of the Church*, published in 1837, in which he proposed the outlines for the special theology of the Anglican Church, the theology of the Via Media. As Newman saw this idea, the Via Media was a middle course between the errors of Roman Catholicism on the one hand, and the errors of Protestantism of the other, and, thus, a return to the Anglicanism of the seventeenth century.

According to Newman, one of the errors of Rome was to utilize a Tradition which was not based solely on the Scriptures. In fact, several of the *Lectures* are devoted to the importance of the supreme authority of Scripture and the recognition of the Apostles' Creed as the sole transmission of Christian doctrine from the Scriptures to the present day. As Newman explained its importance in Lecture XII:

> Next, we learn from the testimony of the early Church, that Scripture and Scripture only is inspired. This explains *how* it may be called in an especial manner the Testament or Will of our Lord and Saviour. Scripture has a gift which Tradition has not; it is fixed, tangible, accessible, readily applicable, and besides all this perfectly true in all its arts and relations; in a word, it is a sacred *text*. Tradition does not convey to us any sacramental words, as they may be called, or sustained discourses, but ideas and things only. It gives us little or nothing which can be handled and argued from. We can argue only from a text; we can argue freely only from an inspired text. Thus Scripture is in itself specially fitted for

---

[9] *Letters and Diaries*, 5:103.

that office which we assign it in our Article; to be a reposi-
tory of manifold and various Doctrine, a means of proof, a
standard of appeal, an umpire and test between truth and
falsehood in all emergencies. It thus becomes the nearest
possible approach to the perpetual presence of the Apostles
in the Church; whereas Tradition, being rather a collection
of separate truths, facts, and usages, is wanting in applicabil-
ity to the subtle questions and difficulties which from time to
time arise. A new heresy, for instance, would be refuted by
Tradition negatively, on the very ground that it was new;
but by Scripture positively, by the use of its text, and by
suitable inferences from it.[10]

But, gradually, Newman began to realize that there were
problems with his concept that only the Scriptures and the
Apostles' Creed were necessary for the complete transmission
of Christian doctrine. He soon came to see that he could not
overlook other elements beyond apostolic Tradition: "The
more he sought to bring out its direct origin from the Apostles,
its total freedom from additions, its even mechanical and sterile
repetition down the centuries, the less could he convince himself that the process comprised and described the living testimony of the martyrs, the conciliar activity of the Magisterium,
the feverish enquiries and assurances of the theologians: in a
word, the vibrant life of faith in the Church." [11]

Thus, Newman was faced with a dilemma. As Father Bouyer
described it: "How, in practice was this true Catholicism, disfig-
ured as it had been by Rome's errors, so called, on the one hand;
lopped and hacked about by the Protestants on the other—how
was this true Catholicism to be recovered? This was a point
concerning which Newman had nothing to offer save his own
experience; but this he conveys in a formula of singular felicity.
It is perhaps as near the truth as any theory ever advanced
regarding the nature and meaning of Tradition." [12]

[10] John Henry Newman, *The Via Media of the Anglican Church*, vol. 1, *Lectures on the Prophetical Office of the Church* (Westminster, Md.: Christian Classics, 1978), 291–292.
[11] Biemer, *Newman on Tradition*, 45.
[12] Louis Bouyer, *Newman: His Life and Spirituality* (New York: P. J. Kenedy & Sons, 1958), 166.

According to Bouyer, Newman's formula acknowledged the existence of two distinct yet inseparable forms in which Tradition could be manifested. One of these forms he called episcopal Tradition and the other prophetical Tradition. Episcopal Tradition consisted of the official formularies of the hierarchy, such as the several creeds. It was an addition to, and an interpretation of, the Scriptures and was committed to writing which made it fixed, bounded, and stereotyped. Its purpose was to conserve and to safeguard the integrity of the original Church.[13]

However, for Newman the prophetical Tradition was both living and life-giving. While not confined to any particular period of time, such Tradition was like life itself, both one and manifold.[14] Newman described this continuous Tradition:

> By continuous Tradition we have received the sacraments embodied in a certain definite form; and by a like Tradition we have received the doctrines also; Scripture may justify both the one and the other, when given, without being sufficient to enable individuals to put into shape whether doctrines or Sacraments, apart from oral teaching and Tradition. Besides, if the Holy Spirit illuminates the Word of God for the use of the individual in all things, then of course as regards unfulfilled prophecy also; which we know is not the case. As then, for all that the Spirit is given us, the event is necessary in order to interpret prophecy, so in like manner a similar external fact may be necessary for understanding doctrine. True then though it be that "the natural man discerneth not the things of the Spirit of God;" it does not therefore follow that the spiritual man discerneth spiritual things through Scripture only, not through Creeds. . . . I conclude that the popular theory of rejecting all other helps and reading the Bible only, though in most cases maintained merely through ignorance, is yet in itself presumptuous.[15]

Bouyer explained further the prophetical Tradition as including the writings of the doctors, the formularies and ritual of

---

[13] See ibid.
[14] Ibid.
[15] Newman, *The Via Media*, 1:166–167.

the liturgies, the continuous teaching of the Church, and the soul of Christians as it expressed itself throughout the whole of their existence. For Newman, the prophetical and episcopal traditions were definitely intertwined. If episcopal Tradition were not at hand to clarify and define it, prophetical Tradition would always be in danger of being overlaid by corruption. "It is the living truth that dwells forever in Christian souls and in the Church. Rather than any catalogue of dogmas and definitions, it is what St. Paul calls 'the mind of the Spirit,' the thought and principle which breathed in the Church, her accustomed and unconscious mode of viewing things." [16]

Because of the experience that he had had in Italy during which he witnessed a vibrant Church that included devotions to Mary and other saints and because of his continual searching for answers, Newman now had a more clearly defined explanation of the value of Catholic Tradition as the heart and soul of the Church. "The spirit, the soul of the Church is not handed on by formal teaching; it is only by dwelling in the *milieu* which is permeated by it, by adopting what is called. . . its ideal of life, that we may make it ours." [17]

Thus, with the publication of *The Via Media*, Newman would enter a new phase in his life. He and the other Tractarians wanted this "ideal of life" to permeate the Anglican Church which they now perceived as tired, uninspired, and ruled by liberals. To this end, they worked even harder to effect this most necessary change, although they were ever-mindful that they should not be led into Roman errors and exaggerations.

> The only way to reach the vast public was to provide them with the incontestable signs of doctrinal, liturgical, and ascetical renewal which would infuse into the Church itself the clear consciousness of its own greatness, its true Tradition and apostolic mission. Therefore, from 1835 to 1839, the Tractarian Movement engaged in study and theological reflection, of which Newman was the most conspicuous

[16] Bouyer, *Newman*, 166–167.
[17] Ibid., 167.

leader. At the same time, his sermons at St. Mary's were drawing the largest and most enthusiastic audiences.[18]

While Newman was facing much controversy as he surged forward, he felt he was truly doing God's work:

> So I went on for years up to 1841. It was, in a human point of view, the happiest time of my life. I was truly at home. I had in one of my volumes appropriated to myself the words of Bramhall, "Bees, by the instinct of nature, do love their hives, and birds their nests." I did not suppose that such sunshine would last, though I knew not what would be its termination. It was the time of plenty, and during its seven years, I tried to lay up as much as I could for the dearth which was to follow it. We prospered and spread. . . .
>
> "From beginnings so small," I said, "from elements of thought so fortuitous, with prospects so unpromising, the Anglo-Catholic party suddenly became a power in the National Church, and an object of alarm to her rulers and friends. . . ." In a very few years a school of opinion was formed, fixed in its principles, indefinite and progressive in their range; and it extended itself into every part of the country. If we inquire what the world thought of it, we have still more to raise our wonder; for, not to mention the excitement it caused in England, the Movement and its party-names were known to the police of Italy and to the backwoodmen [*sic*] of America.[19]

From Italy to America, Newman and his Movement were becoming known as either cause for distress or cause for celebration. Whatever the outcome, Newman was beginning to accept the idea that he was, in fact, an Anglo-Catholic who had some serious issues with the established Church of England.

John Henry Newman and Saint Alfonso Liguori

With John Henry Newman's drawing closer to the Anglo-Catholic position, little by little he seemed to be attempting to discover and understand elements of Catholic Tradition and

---

[18] Ibid., 107.
[19] Newman, *Apologia*, 82–83.

spirituality. In 1841, he published the celebrated Tract 90, which would be his last. In this tract, he developed the idea that the Thirty-Nine Articles, which constitute the charter of the Anglican Church, are in complete agreement with the dogmas of the Council of Trent, "provided the latter are purified of all Roman accretions, which obscure and falsify their original meaning. Such an interpretation of the Thirty-Nine Articles, which too bluntly ran up against Anglican prejudices then so strongly colored by Protestantism, initiated the most vociferous reprobation." [20]

The more suspect Newman and his friends became among their Anglican contemporaries, the more confidently Newman continued to search further for spiritual direction:

> Such was about my state of mind, on the publication of Tract 90 in February, 1841. I was indeed in prudence taking steps towards eventually withdrawing from St. Mary's, and I was not confident about my permanent adhesion to the Anglican creed; but I was in no actual perplexity or trouble of mind. Not did the immense commotion consequent upon the publication of the Tract unsettle me again: for I fancied I had weathered the storm, as far as the bishops were concerned: the Tract had not been condemned: that was the great point, and I made much of it. [21]

At this same period in time, Newman had an on-going correspondence with a young Irish Catholic priest, Charles Russell, who would contribute greatly to Newman's eventual conversion to the Catholic Faith. Charles William Russell was born in Killough, Ireland, in 1812. He went to Maynooth College in 1826 and was ordained a priest there in 1835. That same year he joined the staff of the College and was made Professor of Church History in 1845. A keen student of Leibnitz, he was always searching for signs of Catholic feeling outside the Church, and he followed with great interest the progress of the Oxford Movement. [22]

---

[20] Jean Cardinal Honoré, *The Spiritual Journey of Newman* (New York: Alba House, 1992), 108.

[21] *Apologia*, 131–132.

[22] See Gerard Tracey, ed., "Index of Persons and Places," in *The Letters and Diaries of John Henry Newman*, vol. 8 (Oxford: Clarendon Press, 1999), 637.

In fact, after having read Newman's Tract 90, Russell felt that he needed to object personally to Newman's misrepresentation of the Catholic doctrine of transubstantiation. Their correspondence continued as Russell sought to answer many of Newman's questions calling into doubt the validity behind certain Catholic dogmas and traditions. "A crucial one for Newman that lay at the heart of the Catholic-Anglican divide was the doctrine of the invocation of saints, and of the Roman Catholic devotion to Mary in particular, which Newman dubbed an offense to the 'incommunicable glory' of God." [23]

Russell certainly did help to convince Newman otherwise, and Newman spoke at length about him in the *Apologia*:

> He had, perhaps, more to do with my conversion than any one else. He called upon me, in passing through Oxford in the summer of 1841, and I think I took him over some of the buildings of the University. He called again another summer, on his way from Dublin to London. I do not recollect that he said a word on the subject of religion on either occasion. He sent me at different times several letters; he was always gentle, mild, unobtrusive, uncontroversial. He let me alone. He also gave me one or two books. Vernon's Rule of Faith and some Treatises of the Wallenburghs was one; a volume of St. Alfonso Liguori's Sermons was another; and it is to those Sermons that my letter to Dr. Russell relates.
>
> Now it must be observed that the writings of St. Alfonso, as I knew them by the extracts commonly made from them, prejudiced me as much against the Roman Church as anything else, on account of what was called their "Mariolatry," but there was nothing of the kind in this book. I wrote to ask Dr. Russell whether any thing had been left out in the translation; he answered that there certainly were omissions in one Sermon about the Blessed Virgin. This omission, in the case of a book intended for Catholics, at least showed that such passages as are found in the works of Italian authors were not acceptable to every part of the Catholic world. Such devotional manifestations in honour of Our

---

[23] Nicholas L. Gregoris, *"The Daughter of Eve Unfallen": Mary in the Theology and Spirituality of John Henry Newman* (Mount Pocono, Pa.: Newman House Press, 2003), 366.

Lady had been my great *crux* as regards Catholicism; I say frankly, I do not fully enter into them now; I trust I do not love her the less, because I cannot enter into them. They may be fully explained and defended; but sentiment and taste do not run with logic; they are suitable for Italy, but they are not suitable for England. But, over and above England, my own case was special; from a boy I had been led to consider that my Maker and I, His creature, were the two beings luminously such *in rerum natura.* I will not here speculate, however, about my own feelings. Only this I know full well now, and did not know then, that the Catholic Church allows no image of any sort, material or immaterial, no dogmatic symbol, no rite, no sacrament, no saint, not even the Blessed Virgin herself, to come between the soul and its Creator. It is face to face, *"solus cum solo,"* in all matters between man and his God. He alone creates; He alone has redeemed; before His awful eyes we go in death; in the vision of Him is our eternal beatitude.[24]

This unusually expansive passage in the *Apologia* concerning Charles Russell and St. Alfonso Liguori is indicative of the importance of these two men in Newman's understanding of the Blessed Virgin Mary as an essential element in Catholic Tradition. For the first time in his life, Newman was reading a more complete version of the sermons of the Italian saint Alfonso [Alphonsus de'] Liguori. Liguori's life spanned virtually the whole of the eighteenth century from his birth in 1696 to his death at the age of ninety-one in 1787, just fourteen years before the birth of John Newman. The historical records for Naples, where he lived and worked for the greater part of his life, are extensive. In fact, the houses in which he lived, the cathedrals and rural churches where he preached as both priest and bishop, are to a large extent still in existence. He wrote extensively, and a considerable portion of his works is still extant in manuscript form with Alfonso's corrections and emendations.[25]

---

[24] *Apologia,* 178–179.
[25] See Frederick M. Jones, C.SS.R., ed., *Alphonsus de Liguori: Selected Writings* (New York: Paulist Press, 1999), 9.

By the time Newman had read Liguori, many theologians had already accused the Italian of excesses in Marian piety. However, a fair estimation of the place of Mary in the spirituality of St. Alphonsus must keep two factors in mind:

> First, of the over one hundred works written by Alphonsus, only one, *The Glories of Mary*, is devoted entirely to the Blessed Virgin Mary. Merely on a statistical basis the attention paid by Alphonsus to Our Lady is minor compared to his writings devoted to various aspects of the Person of Jesus the Redeemer. Second, all of Alphonsus's writings must be viewed through the optic of the central choice in his life and ministry—to preach the good news of plentiful redemption to the most abandoned, especially the poor, who have the least recourse to the Church's ordinary ministry. Preaching on the Blessed Virgin Mary was a powerful pastoral instrument for that population. Alphonsus himself remarked that the sinner who remained untouched by sermons on Hell would be moved by a sermon on the Mother of God. Alphonsus's apostolic genius consisted in his ability to use the popular piety of the poor of eighteenth-century Naples as a way of integrating them more fully in the Church's life and of teaching them a more integral spirituality.[26]

In this manner, Liguori could appeal to the poor people of Naples, as well as to John Henry Newman of Oxford. His sermons in *The Glories of Mary* included theological expositions:

> If perhaps some of the statements in this book might seem outlandish to some, I declare that I have made them and understood them in the same sense in which the Holy Catholic Church and sound theology understand them. For example, by calling Mary "mediatrix" I intend to refer to her as a mediatrix of grace in contrast to Jesus, who is the prime and unique mediator of justification. By calling Mary "all-powerful" (as have St. John Damascene, St. Peter Damian, St. Bonaventure, Cosmo Gerosolimitano, and others), I mean this in the sense that as Mother of God she can obtain from God by her prayers whatever she asks in favor on those devoted to her; neither this nor any other divine attribute can properly be applied to a creature, and Mary is

---

[26] Ibid., 239.

but a creature. By calling Mary "our Hope" I intend by this (as taught by St. Bernard) that all graces come to us by her hands.[27]

In addition, Liguori was a master of anecdotal information which he used to increase the piety of the Italian people. He included commonplace stories to emphasize the powers of Mary:

A woman came to one of the houses our little Congregation has in this kingdom to tell one of our priests that her husband had not been to confession in many years. The unhappy woman was at her wits' end to think what more she could do to convince him. If she so much as mentioned confession, he would beat her. The priest instructed the woman to give him a picture of Mary Immaculate. When evening came, the woman once again begged her husband to go to confession. As usual he pretended to be deaf and so she gave him the picture. He had barely received the picture when he said, "Well, I'm ready. When are you going to take me to confession?" The woman, seeing such an instantaneous change, began to weep for joy. In the morning he came to our church. When the Redemptorist asked him how long it had been since his last confession, he answered, "Twenty-eight years." "How is it," asked the priest, "that you felt moved this morning to come to confession?" "Father," he said, "I was stubborn. Last night my wife gave me a picture of the Madonna and immediately I felt my heart change. Throughout the night every moment seemed a thousand years to me, so anxious was I for the day to arrive so that I could go to confession." He then went to confession with great compunction, changed his life, and continued to go frequently to confession to the same Father.[28]

After having read many of the sermons and anecdotal examples of St. Alfonso, Newman was surprised to find none of the idolatry or superstition that he had expected to encounter. Put back into their proper context, some of the expressions which Liguori's opponents had cited seemed devoid of offence,

[27] Ibid., 248.
[28] Ibid., 259.

and the narrative stories made sense in Newman's mind as important teaching tools in an Italian society where many people were totally illiterate. "Moreover, he came to see that, when viewed against their national background, even the most seemingly extravagant of these popular devotional practices involved nothing that was necessarily incompatible with fundamental Christianity." [29] These types of devotions might not be to the taste of an English theologian, but they were part of Italian Catholic Tradition, and they could not be regarded "as presenting a serious argument against the Church which tolerated them." [30]

In fact, Meriol Trevor, in her book *Newman: The Pillar of the Cloud*, has written of Liguori that he could almost be called a Catholic Wesley. She explained that Newman was surprised to find what a distorted view the Protestant writers had given of the Italian saint. "His fears about corruptions were already allayed by habitual reading of the sober Breviary offices, but here was evidence from the popular and contemporary side that Mary and the Pope were not presented as substitutes for Christ but had their own places in the scheme of redemption." [31]

In *Newman: Il Coraggio della Verità*, the Reverend Giovanni Velocci, C.SS.R., explained the significance of St. Alfonso Liguori in the development of Newman's thoughts:

> Newman knew that this saint [Alphonsus de' Ligouri] was held by Anglicans to be the greatest representative of devotional Catholicism, of "Mariolatry," and that Saint Alphonsus had fed his prejudices against Catholicism. But this book was a surprise and a revelation: Newman did not find in it the exaggerated devotions that he feared, but on the contrary a serious and concrete doctrine, even if presented with the mentality and warmth of an Italian. . . . Saint Alphonsus Liguori had played a considerable role in enlightening and bringing to the true Church the most illustrious convert of the nineteenth century. . . .

[29] Bouyer, *Newman*, 224.
[30] Ibid.
[31] Meriol Trevor, *Newman: The Pillar of the Cloud* (London: Macmillan & Co., 1962), 285.

Our exposition shows that Newman considered Saint
Alphonsus essentially from two points of view: as a saint and
as a writer. Newman had an unconditional admiration for
the saint, took him as a model, felt him to be his protector,
frequently turned to him in prayer, especially in the difficult
moments of life. For Saint Alphonsus the writer, Newman
had a noteworthy and constant interest, but he also had
reservations: Newman approached Saint Alphonsus with
freedom and with a critical sense, rejected some of his opinions, accepted others, followed him in the solution of pastoral problems and in cases of conscience. But Newman, his
whole life long, maintained a certain debt of gratitude to
Saint Alphonsus, because he had received from him a decisive impetus to detach himself from Anglicanism and to
orient himself toward the Catholic Church in order to enter
into the fullness of light and truth.[32]

Thus, the works of Liguori did much to orient Newman
towards Catholicism and, specifically, to convince him that the
veneration of Mary and the saints was not the heterodoxy that
he had once thought it to be. Father Bouyer made a perceptive
summation of Newman's thinking after discovering Liguori:

These very simple discoveries, coming, as they did, at the
psychological moment, put a different face on the problem.
Henceforth the ground was cleared, and the two Churches
stood face to face, fairly and squarely. No more preconcep-
tions now for either of them, favourable or unfavourable.
Doubtless, Newman, always so keenly on the look-out for
the signs of Providence, was not to quit the Church of his
baptism till he had made quite sure that it was his duty to
do so, but, at any rate, whether he was to go, or to remain
where he was, was now a legitimately debatable question.[33]

The Aftermath of Tract 90

Although Newman was confident that he had weathered well
the conflict brought about by the publication of his Tract 90,

---

[32] Giovanni Velocci, C.SS.R., *Newman: Il Coraggio della Verità* (Vatican City: Libreria Editrice Vaticana, 2000), 199–214.
[33] Bouyer, *Newman*, 224.

the reactions against it were widespread and clamorous. As Cardinal Honoré described the response:

> It is difficult to imagine how violent was the indignation that shook the common rooms of the University after the publication of the Tract. For many, Newman and his friends were already suspect since the publication of the preceding tracts, and above all, since the edition of the posthumous papers of Froude. . . .
>
> The name of Newman became synonymous with that of a Romanist: he became a sign of contradiction; his disgrace was such that his name was posted on the refectory doors of the colleges! His cause was lost. In spite of the generous efforts of Keble and Pusey, Newman was definitely compromised in the eyes of the bishops. It was already the signal of death for the Movement and sanctions were taken against a certain number of Newmanians. Pusey himself was accused of Romanism for a sermon he preached on the Eucharist, in which he proclaimed his faith in the Real Presence. Newman, a prey to the most mortal agony of his conscience, retired from Oxford and took refuge in a hermitage, a few miles away from Oxford, in the little parish of Littlemore.[34]

At this point, Newman was feeling guilty for having involved his friends in his own personal spiritual journey. His only recourse seemed to be a withdrawal from the public life and a continuation of his scholarly endeavors in isolation at Littlemore. He was in the process of reading Liguori, who would help him to appreciate the Catholic Tradition of piety towards Mary and the Saints. However, he had not as yet grasped the concept of the transmission of Tradition. "Up to this, Newman had really envisaged only the mechanical concept of Tradition which was generally in vogue. He had cherished the idea that formulas verbally identical had been handed on, and that this repetition had assured the essential identity of the doctrine." [35] In order to understand further the development of doctrine and Tradition, Newman once again turned to the Church Fathers. As he described this most difficult year:

[34] Honoré, *Spiritual Journey of Newman*, 108.
[35] Biemer, *Newman on Tradition*, 51–52.

In the summer of 1841, I found myself at Littlemore, without any harass or anxiety on my mind. I had determined to put aside all controversy, and I set myself down to my translation of St. Athanasius; but, between July and November, I received three blows which broke me.

1. I had got but a little way in my work, when my trouble returned on me. The ghost had come a second time. In the Arian history I found the very same phenomenon, in a far bolder shape, which I had found in the Monophysite. I had not observed it in 1832. Wonderful that this should come upon me! I had not sought it out. I was reading and writing in my own life of study, far from the controversies of the day, on what is called a "metaphysical" subject; but I saw clearly, that in the history of Arianism, the pure Arians were the Protestants, the semi-Arians were the Anglicans, and that Rome now was what it was then. The truth lay, not with the Via Media, but with what was called "the extreme party."

2. I was in the misery of this new unsettlement when a second blow came upon me. The Bishops, one after another, began to charge against me. It was a formal, determinate movement. This was the real understanding; that on which I had acted on the first appearance of Tract Ninety, had come to nought. I think the words which had then been used to me were, that "perhaps two or three of them might think it necessary to say something in their charges;" but by this time they had tided over the difficulty of the Tract, and there was no one to enforce the understanding. They went on in this way, directing charges at me, for three whole years. I recognized it as a condemnation; it was the only one that was in their power. . . .

3. As if this were not enough, there came the affair of the Jerusalem Bishopric. . . . At the very time that the Anglican Bishops were directing their censures upon me for avowing an approach to the Catholic Church not closer than I believed the Anglican formularies would allow, they were, on the other hand, fraternizing, by their act or by their sufferance, with Protestant bodies, and allowing them to put themselves under an Anglican Bishop, without any renunciation of their errors, or regard to their due reception of Baptism and Confirmation; while there was great reason to suppose that the said Bishop was intended to make converts from the orthodox Greeks and the schismatical Oriental

bodies, by means of the influence of England. This was the third blow, which finally shattered my faith in the Anglican Church. That Church was not only forbidding any sympathy or concurrence with the Church of Rome, but it actually was courting an intercommunion with Protestant Prussia and the heresy of the Orientals. The Anglican Church might have the apostolical succession, as had the Monophysites, but such acts as were in progress led me to the gravest suspicion, not that it would soon cease to be a Church, but that, since the 16th century, it had never been a Church all along. . . .

As to the project of a Jerusalem Bishopric, I never heard of any good or harm it has ever done, except what it has done for me, which many think a great misfortune, and I one of the greatest of mercies. It brought me on to the beginning of the end.[36]

---

[36] *Apologia*, 33–140.

IV

BLESSED DOMINIC BARBERI AND THE CONVERSION

Newman and Father Dominic Barberi

Newman ended his long discourse on the three blows which broke him with the ominous statement that from the end of 1841 he was on his "death-bed" regarding his belonging to the Anglican Church.[1] Yet, in true Newman fashion, he also expressed hope in the future with the acknowledgment that Dr. Russell had introduced him to the writings of the Italian saint, Alfonso Liguori, and he was thinking very seriously about the concepts that he was learning from Liguori. Coincidentally, at that same time there was in England another Italian, Father Dominic Barberi, who would eventually become world-famous for converting John Henry Newman to Catholicism.

In the ceremony of the beatification of Dominic Barberi on 27 October 1963, Pope Paul VI linked together Blessed Dominic and Newman as "the two saintly figures."[2] There can be no doubt that both of these "saintly" men were much taken with each other, although Barberi was probably aware of Newman's importance long before Newman had ever heard of Dominic Barberi. However, later on, Newman was to admire how the poor Italian priest had risen from the most humble of origins:

> He was a poor boy, who (I believe) kept sheep near Rome and from his youth his thoughts have been most singularly and distinctly turned to the conversion of England. He is a shrewd clever man, but as unaffected and simple as a child;

[1] *Apologia*, 141.
[2] Christopher Hollis, *Newman and the Modern World* (Garden City, N.Y.: Doubleday & Co., 1968), 7.

and most singularly kind in his thoughts of religious persons
in our communion. I wish all persons were as charitable as I
know him to be. After waiting near thirty years, suddenly his
superiors sent him to England, without any act of his own.
However, he has not laboured in conversions, but confined
himself to missions and retreats among his own people. I
believe him to be a very holy man.[3]

That "holy man," Dominic (Domenico) Barberi, was born in
a small village near Viterbo, Italy, on June 22, 1792, just eight
years before the birth of Newman himself. Most of what is
known today about the life of Father Barberi has been collected
in a definitive biography by Denis Gwynn, who has incorpo-
rated all relevant earlier materials. In fact, on the title page of
his book, Gwynn used the following quote in which Newman
strongly expressed his esteem for the Italian priests who had
come as missionaries to England: "If they want to convert
England, let them go barefooted into our manufacturing
towns—let them preach to the people like St. Francis Xavier—
let them be pelted and trampled on, and I will own that they
can do what we cannot. I confess they are our betters, far."[4]

One can only speculate that Newman might have felt more
comfortable being converted by an Italian priest than by a
native-born Catholic, but there can be no doubt that he was
taken by the personage of Dominic Barberi and by the work
that he had done in England. For Newman, Father Barberi was
the personification of the Catholic missionary. Barberi, an
Italian, had done what Newman's own countrymen were not
capable of doing. In the Catholic Tradition of the missionary,
Barberi had devoted his life to the propagation of the Christian
Faith in a land where there was a marked decline in true belief.
He had modeled himself on all of those great Italian missionaries and saints who had gone before him, and he gave the
remainder of his life to a country and a people who were not his
own. Undoubtedly, Newman's concepts of the sacrifices and

---

[3] Newman, "To Mrs J. W. Bowden," Oct. 8, 1845, *Letters and Diaries*, 11:5.
[4] Denis Gwynn, *Father Dominic Barberi* (Buffalo, N.Y.: Desmond & Stapleton, 1948),
iii.

accomplishments of a true missionary were based on his knowledge of the life of Dominic Barberi and the personal statements that Barberi made to him as their friendship developed.

And, in fact, the story of Barberi's life is quite remarkable. He had been born to a poor family of farmers, and both his parents were dead by the time he was eight years old. He never attended school, and taught himself to read and write. Napoleon was in possession of northern Italy at that time, and he closed all of the Italian religious houses. However, Dominic became acquainted with several Passionist priests living in exile at Merlano, and they invited him to pray with them.[5]

One day, he went into the church while the others were eating, and he knelt before the altar of the Blessed Virgin. In his own words, at that moment the plan for his life became evident:

> Was I to go as a lay-brother to preach and to whom was I to go? Where was I to go? China and America came into my mind. Suddenly, in the twinkling of an eye, I understood (not by an interior voice but by another and more elevated mode of communication which I cannot explain) that I was not to remain a lay-brother any longer, but to begin my studies as a cleric forthwith, and enter after six years, on the apostolic ministry. Further, I understood that I was to labour, not in China or America, but in North-West Europe, and especially in England. The exact time was not made clear to me, and neither was the manner in which I was to be sent there. I was so convinced of this being a divine communication that I would have sooner doubted my own existence than its truth, and its eventual fulfillment at the hands of His Divine Majesty.[6]

This "divine communication" would lead Barberi far from Italy and would inspire him in a manner that would affect the future of Catholicism in England. As Cardinal Henry Edward Manning wrote many years later: "The memory of Father Dominic, who in the mountains of Italy felt his heart burn within him to preach the Passion of Jesus Christ in England, will

[5] See ibid., 11–13.
[6] Ibid., 15.

ever be dear to us. His apostolate among us was short, but it had abundant fruit. It was he whom God chose to bring into the Catholic unity many of the first-fruits of the return to the Faith in England." [7]

However, the road to England would not be an easy one for Barberi. On 14 November 1814, at the age of twenty-two, he joined the Passionist Order and was ordained a priest four years later. At this point, he was already rather older than the students of his own group, and he still had three more years of study in Rome before he was to finish his schooling.[8] His own training was followed by years of teaching and writing, and in 1831 he became Rector of the new Passionist Retreat at Lucca. But Barberi had never abandoned his longing to go to England, and while in Rome he had met the Englishman, George Spencer, who was a convert to Catholicism and who would afterward become one of Barberi's Passionist priests in the English provinces. "Through their intimate friendship Dominic Barberi came to know Msgr. Wiseman, Rector of the English College in Rome, and he became intensely interested in the desire of the Tractarians to restore Catholic traditions within the Church of England. But his election as Provincial of the Passionists in Italy made the prospect of his going to England seem more than ever remote." [9]

However, through it all, Barberi never ceased to refer from time to time to his future work in England, almost as though he was already under orders to go there. He certainly possessed the true zeal of the missionary if not the tools, for he did not speak English, and he could barely read any letters or works in English. "Yet, one day, when he had narrowly escaped drowning as he rode across a swollen river on the way to give a retreat, he explained, after he had arrived safely, that he 'had never

---

[7] Henry Edward Manning, in *Dominic Barberi in England: A New Series of Letters*, ed. Father Urban Young (London: Burns Oates & Washbourne, 1935), vii. Manning was first a High Anglican and then became a strong force in the Catholic Church in England.

[8] See Gwynn, *Father Dominic Barberi*, 18.

[9] Ibid., 18.

really thought of death. You see, I have to go to England, where I shall die, and not elsewhere.'" [10] How much he reminds one of Newman, who, also, could not die in Sicily, for he, too, still had work to do in England!

Father Dominic persevered, and his position as the head of a Passionist foundation in Belgium led to a mission in England which finally fulfilled his hopes of so many years. On Guy Fawkes Day, November 1840, Barberi landed in England, and "ignorant of English ways began his work by doing just what Newman had required, going barefoot into the manufacturing towns in his monk's habit and preaching in broken English to any one who would listen, with surprising success. But he was pelted too, with mud and stones." [11]

Soon after he arrived in England, Barberi saw for himself how extreme was the division that existed within the Anglican Church and, also, the profound influence of the Oxford Movement. As he wrote in a letter dated 9 February 1841:

> I have acquired a good deal of information myself during my visits to London and Oscott, and also whilst a guest in the house of Mr. Phillipps. [12] The Anglican Church (at present the dominating religious body) has been for a long time divided into two great parties—the Low Church, or ultra-Protestant, and intensely opposed to Catholicism, and the High Church, or Oxford party. They are thus called for the reason that the majority of the leading men of the Oxford University are adherents of this section, of which they are, so to say, the soul and centre. This party has been in existence for a long time, and increases daily in numbers and esteem from outsiders. Now, all the members of this party are most friendly to us, and I might almost term them Catholics in heart. Not only are they most anxious to unite themselves to the centre of Catholic truth, but they long to bring with them the whole of the great British Empire, which extends

---

[10] Ibid., 45.

[11] Meriol Trevor, *Newman: The Pillar of the Cloud* (Garden City, N.Y.: Doubleday & Co., 1962), 252–253.

[12] Ambrose Phillipps was a friend of George Spencer. The heir of a wealthy family, he became a Catholic at the age of fifteen. He was excited about the Oxford Movement and hoped for a Catholic England once again.

into the four quarters of the globe. These men are most edified by the fervour of Catholics, who pray for the conversion of England. They thank us and exhort us to pray with ever increasing fervour, saying "Let us pray together; let us pray that there may be one fold and one shepherd." . . . They all venerate Catholic practices, observe the fasts of the Church, and very many recite the Breviary. Of the clerics, many observe celibacy and are devout to the Blessed Virgin and the saints. . .

Nor is all this enough: they do more. For some years they have been publishing, at regular intervals, very fine works in defense of the Catholic Church [The *Tracts for the Times*]. Among others they brought out some time ago are excellent treatises on the necessity of Tradition. With this as foundation they are continuing the examination and analysis of all the dogmas and practices of the Church, demonstrating as they advance, in the clearest possible way, that these dogmas and practices come down from the Apostles and the Fathers of the primitive Church.[13]

With England in such a religious turmoil, Father Dominic appeared on the scene, and despite any expectations on his part, he would ultimately become a purveyor of traditional Catholicism. At first, however, he was a less than imposing figure, for he was an Italian, and he spoke English with difficulty. He and his few missionaries were among the first in England since the Reformation to wear religious habits publicly, and they were constantly reminded that their actions inflamed hostility towards them. During Holy Week one year, he had deliberately preached "exactly as in Italy" which included a habit with the crucifix on the breast. "Timid Catholics used to implore him to avoid such provocation, but he preferred to listen to those who told him that 'the wearing of the sandals seemed to give great edification,' and advised him 'to wear both habit and sandals on all future occasions of the kind.'"[14]

At this point, the discreet Newman would probably have been averse to any kind of public association with Father

---

[13] Dominic Barberi, quoted in Gwynn, *Dominic Barberi*, 39–42, and *passim*.
[14] Ibid., xiv.

Dominic, an Italian man who openly and proudly observed the traditions of his Order and his faith. But, as can be seen by his early life, Dominic was a man of conviction and tenacity, and he had heard from third parties of the illustrious Dr. Newman and was determined to meet him. In midsummer of 1844, he gave a mission in a hayloft near Heythrop, a location not far from Littlemore. This proximity was the opportunity that the Italian had been waiting for to pay a visit to Newman and his community:

> He [Barberi] had been corresponding, intermittently with Dalgairns[15] ever since that young man had written a letter about the Movement, in French, to the *Univers* . . . It was only a few years since he had come to England, and he was fifty-two. He had given up his habit now, and wore a scratch lot of black clothes, old patched boots and an ancient hat. He was short, with a round face, and keen eyes. "His very look had about it something holy," Newman wrote long after. "When his form came in sight I was moved to the depths of my being in the strangest way. The gaiety and affability of his manner in the midst of all his sanctity was in itself a holy sermon." Father Dominic was delighted with Littlemore, with the poverty and simplicity of the house, and with its inhabitants. He went away, back to his arduous life, preaching in broken English to all who would listen. In him for the first time Newman met what he had told Ambrose Phillipps he saw no sign of in the Roman Catholic Church, holiness in action.[16]

Thus, for the first time and in the person of a humble Italian missionary, John Henry Newman saw that true "holiness in action" did exist within the Catholic Church. Of course, although he was simple and unaffected, Dominic was not shy, and he took this first meeting as an opportunity to further his relationship with the residents of Littlemore. In the period immediately afterwards, he saw Newman frequently, and he described Newman very much as the latter had viewed him.

---

[15] John Dobree Dalgairns was a young don at Exeter College who had acquired an important position among Newman's followers.

[16] Trevor, *Newman: The Pillar*, 324.

According to Dominic, Newman was "in my judgement one of the most humble and lovable men I have met in my life." [17]

At the same time, Father Dominic's reputation was growing, and the man who, three years before could not speak two words of English, was now being recognized as a threat by the Protestants. As he reported: "They preach in their churches at the same hour as I do, to keep people from coming to hear me. They have started house to house visiting, with the sole object of exhorting the people not to come to me. . . . I hear that they are afraid and have some idea that I am a very learned person." With keen insight he added, "to make Catholics is not easy, for the good reason that they have to be made Christians first, and that is precisely the difficulty." [18]

Barberi saw his mission as one of converting the High Anglicans who had followed Newman and were now watching carefully to see whether Newman himself would go towards Rome. Gradually, Father Dominic's success in attracting Protestants became extraordinary, and a year before Newman's conversion, the Italian drew over a thousand attendees at a Corpus Christi procession, of whom half were Protestants. "We are called upon from all sides," he wrote. "If I had a dozen missionaries at my disposal I could use them all. Through want of time and men I am forced to refuse many requests for missions, etc." [19]

As the number of Catholics in England swelled by the tens of thousands, Father Dominic needed more and more help. He reported that about 40,000 Catholics had not made their Easter duty because there were not enough priests to hear their confessions. However, this rapid increase was not due in large part to the Oxford Movement or to conversions in England but to the steadily growing influx of emigrant Catholics from Ireland. That influx was to increase with great momentum when the famine in Ireland started in 1845—the year of Newman's con-

[17] Gwynn, *Dominic Barberi*, xv.
[18] Barberi, quoted in *Dominic Barberi*, xv-xvi.
[19] Ibid., xvi–xvii.

version—and continued for several more years. And to make matters worse, with the new Irish immigrants came an outbreak of the plague.[20]

But Barberi and his missionaries were not to be deterred, and the sacrifices made by them on behalf of those unfortunate Irish Catholics had a marked effect upon the English people. By the following February, Father Dominic reported again about the need for more help:

> Here in England not a week passes without the death of some priests, stricken down by the plague. No Passionist has died so far, but I very much fear the year will not pass without someone being sacrificed. There are so few priests in England now! If we go on this way there will soon be none left. And what then will become of our hopes for the conversion of England? And yet God will not fail to raise up "sons to Abraham." If only you would send me a few more good subjects from Italy! They would not find pleasure, ease, comfort here, but a vast field of labour for the divine glory; and at the end, death, it may be, amid suffering and pain.[21]

And so it was to be with Father Dominic Barberi. The strain of so many trials, sufferings, and endeavors in a foreign country had worn out his strength. For many years, he had been almost crippled with many ailments and with the deprivations of his ascetic life. Furthermore, the Irish immigration had overwhelmed the resources of his small community. However, his work had not been in vain, and in one of his last letters before his death, he wrote that there were already three Passionist houses in England—one in Staffordshire, one in Gloucestershire, and one near London. He had twenty-eight religious in England, of whom eleven were already priests. They had by that time given some two-hundred and fifty missions, a hundred of which Father Dominic had done himself. They had converted numerous Protestants to Catholicism and brought thousands of lapsed Catholics back to the Faith. Personally, Father Dominic had received John Henry Newman into the Church of

---

[20] See ibid., xvii.
[21] Ibid., xviii.

Rome. But, by summer of 1849, he realized that he had "finished his course." Within less than a month, Father Dominic Barberi collapsed in a railway train at Pangbourne on his way back to his new foundation in London, and he died within a few hours, on 27 August 1849.[22]

Life at Littlemore from 1841 to 1845

Cardinal Nicholas Wiseman discerned at an early stage that Father Dominic Barberi was perhaps the most symbolic figure of the Catholic revival in England. He often mentioned that while he [Wiseman] was Rector of the English College in Rome or Coadjutor to Bishop Walsh, Father Dominic was devoting all of his thoughts and prayers to the task of reviving the Catholic Church in England.[23] For this work in England and for his role in the conversion of John Henry Newman, Father Dominic Barberi was declared blessed by Pope Paul VI in 1963.

However, during those years that Father Dominic was most active in his English ministry, Newman was keeping himself at a distance from Oxford. He wrote that Tract 90 caused a great crisis and opened an entirely different scene. From the date of publication of the Tract in February 1841, Newman and the members of his group were suspected of Romanism and of dishonesty in saying that they were supporting the Anglican Church and its Thirty-nine Articles. On the contrary, Newman strongly disagreed, as he wrote in the *Apologia*:

> The great stumbling block lay in the 39 Articles. It was urged that here was a positive Note *against* Anglicanism: Anglicanism claimed to hold, that the Church of England was nothing else than a continuation in this country, (as the Church of Rome might be in France or Spain,) of that one Church of which in old times Athanasius and Augustine were members. But, if so, the doctrine must be the same; the doctrine of the Old Church must live and speak in Anglican

---

[22] Ibid., xix.
[23] Denis Gwynn, "Father Dominic Barberi and Cardinal Wiseman," *Westminster Cathedral Chronicle*, 34 (1945): 178.

formularies, in the 39 Articles. Did it? Yes, it did; that is what I maintained; it did in substance, in a true sense. Man had done his worst to disfigure, to mutilate, the old Catholic Truth; but there it was, in spite of them, in the Articles still.[24]

As the early Newman biographer Wilfred Ward explained: "Such a claim amazed the Oxford of 1841, and Newman was charged with dishonest quibbling, a charge which remained in the public mind for many years. . . . The Bishop of Oxford sent a formal message objecting to the Tract and advising the suspension of the series of 'Tracts for the Times.'"[25] But the Bishops were not satisfied with the suspension of the Tracts, and one after another, they issued charges against them which emphasized the Protestant character of the Church of England. In addition, there was the establishment of the strongly Protestant English bishopric in Jerusalem for the express purpose of ruling the Lutheran and Calvinistic congregations of the East.[26]

Besides the actions of the ecclesiastical authorities, events were taking place at Oxford that reminded Newman and his friends that they were regarded with suspicion at the University itself. A description of these happenings helps to explain the frustration that Newman must have felt and the motivation behind his desire to remove himself from the situation:

> Mr. Isaac Williams, who was obviously the best qualified candidate for the Professorship of Poetry left vacant by Keble's resignation, was in January 1842 defeated, unmistakably on the ground of his being a Puseyite, though he was by no means in sympathy with the Romanising wing of the party. Then again in May 1843 Dr. Pusey preached a sermon on the Eucharist. He went not a step beyond the recognized Anglican divines, and yet was forthwith suspended for two years from preaching, by authority of the Vice-Chancellor. Signs were accumulating on every side that Oxford and the Church of England regarded Tractarianism as necessarily Roman. . . . Newman's doubts

---

[24] *Apologia*, 126.

[25] Wilfred Ward, *The Life of John Henry Cardinal Newman*, vol. 1 (London: Longmans, Green, and Co., 1912), 72–73.

[26] Ibid., 1:74.

perforce revived. How, he asked himself, could a position be normal to the Church of England which its authoritative organs energetically repudiated? Newman's position at Oxford became more and more difficult, and his visits to Littlemore grew longer and longer. Knowing fully the weight of his lightest word, filled with a painful sense of responsibility, speech became almost impossible for him. He had led the party on for years in supreme confidence that he was strengthening the Anglican Church against Rome. He had denounced Rome with energy in his writings. Now, in his uncertainty, he could neither urge his followers to advance towards Rome nor keep back those who were actually moving Romewards. For himself, external events were slowly but surely pressing him onwards. For others he declined all responsibility.[27]

These were times of great uncertainty for Newman. He was exploring new concepts of Catholic Tradition and attempting to incorporate them into his long-held religious beliefs. And, yet, his Anglican superiors were condemning him for his actions and moving more and more in a direction away from Rome and Catholicism. As he told his sister Jemima on 16 November 1841:

The Jerusalem matter is miserable and has given me *great* uneasiness. At length (what no one yet knows of) I have delivered in a formal Protest to my Bishop, which, when it comes to be known, will make a stir. It is to the effect that I consider the measure, if carried out, as removing the Church from her present position and tending to her disorganization.

I do not believe I can be touched for it; and I have not any intention of doing anything more. But future events are quite beyond us. I assure you I fully purpose, having done this, to sit quite still.

Do not believe any absurd reports. They talk in the papers of secessions among us to Rome. Do not believe it. Not one will go. At the same time I cannot answer for *years hence*, if the present state of things is persevered in. The Heads are refus-

[27] Ibid., 1:74–75, *passim*.

ing testimonials for Orders. The effect in time will be to throw a number of young men on the world.

Again, if the whole Church speaks against me, if the Bishops, one by one, &c. &c., of course the effect ultimately will be very fearful.[28]

Newman did just what he had told his sister that he would do, and he sat "quite still." On 19 April 1842, after much deliberation, he moved for good to his cottage at Littlemore. From that time on, it would become his headquarters—his home, his library, and his office—and visits to Oriel were only very occasional. "He was at Littlemore for some days quite alone, without friend or servant. He had made his determination and begun his preparations in February. It is clear that he regarded it as a significant step. The movement had never been more influential, and Tract 90 had an immense sale. But its success was not for him." [29]

Again, Newman confided in his sister Jemima on 6 February 1842:

I am going up to Littlemore [i.e., for good] and my books are all in motion—part gone; the rest in a day or two. It makes me very downcast: it is such a nuisance taking steps. But for years three lines of Horace have been in my ears:

> *Lusisti satis, edisti satis atque bibisti;*
> *Tempus abire tibi est; ne potum largius aequo*
> *Rideat et pulset lasciva decentius aetas.*

Of Tract No. 90, 12,500 copies have been sold, and a third edition is printed. An American clergyman, who was here lately, told me he saw it in every house.[30]

But despite the isolation, the years at Littlemore were to be very productive ones for Newman. Rather than bemoaning his situation, he followed his earlier motto—"Growth is the only evidence of life" [31] —and continued his quest to describe and evaluate the dynamic or evolutionary element in the transmission

---

[28] Newman, "To Mrs. J. Mozley," 325–326.
[29] Ward, *Life of . . . Newman*, 75.
[30] To Mrs. J. Mozley, *Letters and Diaries*, 2:345.
[31] *Apologia*, 26.

of Christine doctrine which he had explored in his *Lectures on the Prophetical Office of the Church.* After the turmoil of Tract 90, Newman gave his deliberate attention for the first time to the principle which had preoccupied him indirectly and incidentally for years—the process of transmitting Tradition. "And perhaps it had pursued him because he had never been able to confront it face to face. It seems that from 1842 on, Newman, impelled by the need for continuity and consistency which was the bent of his own mind, and constrained by external circumstances, set himself to draw the conclusions from his actual premises." [32]

And within his own life, Newman had already witnessed concrete examples of the handing down of Catholic Tradition. He had been befriended by Gennaro who, as Jesus had taught, took a dying stranger and nursed him back to life. From Alphonsus Liguori, he had learned that the Blessed Mother could be seen as the prototype of the true Christian and of true Chrisitanity. And, with the introduction of Father Dominic Barberi into his life, Newman had witnessed the teaching of both formal and informal tenets of the Catholic religion. For Barberi preached Catholicism to the masses as no Englishman could do, while at the same time, he practiced austerity and sacrifice in his daily life. These three Italians taught, and John Henry Newman learned.

In addition, Newman was writing and delivering many sermons, and these processes gave him further opportunities to explore the various aspects of Christian Tradition. In a sermon on St. Andrew's Day in 1841, he said:

> Let us consider the question: Had there been any age of the Church when it might be hoped that the doctrines of the Gospel would have produced their full and legitimate effects, it might have been expected in the primitive age. . . . Yet how different is the case! We need but read the Epistles of St. Paul and the other Apostles to be painfully convinced of the numerous irregularities existing even in the primitive Church. . . . If such, alas, was the Church in the Apostles'

[32] Günter Biemer, *Newman on Tradition* (New York: Herder and Herder, 1967), 51.

age—will this world ever contain more than at best but a mixture of good and truth with its own evil? God indeed *might* make this world an earthly paradise of saints.—But the question is not what He can do, but what He *will* do; and since He never, not even in the apostolic age, excluded vice and heresy from the Christian body, it is at first sight unlikely He ever will.[33]

Once Newman acknowledged that there was corruption and heresy in every age of Christianity, he utilized additional sermons to discuss means by which the true Church could preserve as purely as possible the revelation entrusted to it. Thus, Newman came to realize that the process of transmission was dynamic and could come by various means. "Up to this, Newman had really envisaged only the mechanical concept of Tradition which was generally in vogue. He had cherished the idea that formulas verbally identical had been handed on, and this repetition had assured the essential identity of the doctrine. In reality, however, that is, in the historical reality of man, things were different. Here it was actually necessary that a system of ideas should change in order to remain the same." [34]

In 1843, Newman wrote to a friend that he definitely believed that the Roman Catholic Church was the Church of the Apostles. He explained to his sister, "I do despair of the Church of England, and am so evidently cast off by her, and on the other hand, I am so drawn to the Church of Rome, that I think it *safer*, as a matter of honesty, *not* to keep my living." [35] As Wilfred Ward described those tumultuous days:

England was in schism. . . . He resigned the vicarage of St. Mary's on September 18. In the same year in the pages of the *Conservative Journal* he retracted all his attacks on the Church of Rome. The inevitable sequel was in sight for others as well as for himself—the parting from so many Oxford friends and disciples who had for years hung on his every word. On September 25, he preached at Littlemore

[33] John Henry Newman, *Sermons 1824–1843*, ed. Vincent Blehl, S.J., vol. 2 (Oxford: Clarendon Press, 1993), 337–338,

[34] Biemer, *Newman on Tradition*, 51–52.

[35] Newman, "To Mrs. Thomas Mozley," *Letters and Diaries*, 2:380.

his sermon on the Parting of Friends. It was the last public scene of the silent tragedy which was being enacted. He told in that sermon, clearly for those who understood, how he himself had found the Church of his birth and of his early affections wanting; how he was torn asunder between the claims of those he must leave behind him and those who would follow him; that he could speak to his friends no more from that pulpit, but could only commit them to God and bid them strive to do His will. His voice broke (so the tradition runs), and his words were interrupted by the sobs of his hearers as he said his last words of farewell. . . . From this time onwards he lived in seclusion at Littlemore with a group of his younger disciples, in whose company, he led a life of quasi-monastic discipline.[36]

These words were written in 1912, a little over twenty years after the death of Newman, and the poignancy felt in them is quite apparent. Newman had wanted so much to believe that the Anglican Church had properly transmitted Christian Tradition. "Sanctity has been, he maintained, throughout Church history the great antidote to corruption. His last despairing hope for the Church of England seems to have been that this might be so again, and that, as with the human body, intense vitality might remedy functional disorder and restore normal health." [37]

In view of the fact that Newman finally accepted in his mind the idea that the Anglican Church had not transmitted Christian doctrine without corruption, he began to turn his attention to the existential question: "Where had the development of Christian doctrine been carried out truly and without corruption? Are there external criteria which serve to test an unbroken line of development? [38] Thus, during those days at Littlemore, Newman was very taken up with working on what would become his *Essay on the Development of Christian Doctrine*, which would attempt to answer those questions. According to Bouyer, the *Essay* would, ultimately, become "the work of an Anglican who,

---

[36] Wilfred Ward, *Life of . . . Newman*, 1:76.
[37] Ibid., 1:77.
[38] Biemer, *Newman on Tradition*, 54.

starting from principles which he himself had chosen to lay down, had been led step by step, in the light of his own reasoning, to find his destination in the Church of Rome." [39]

Newman began his *Essay* by saying that "Christianity has been long enough in the world to justify us in dealing with it as a fact in the world's history," and his intention was "directed towards a solution of the difficulty. . . . of our using in controversy the testimony of our most natural informant concerning the doctrine and worship of Christianity, viz., the history of eighteen hundred years." [40] The difficulty, of course, was for Newman to show that despite the fact that Christianity had undergone so many changes over the centuries, there still could be a continuity of doctrine since the time of the Apostles. An inability to reconcile changes and stability has led Protestants to eliminate historical Christianity altogether and to form a Christianity from the Bible alone. [41]

Newman further explained that the famous dictum of Vincent of Lérins to which Anglicans have appealed—"Christianity is what has been held always, everywhere, and by all" [42] —was basically too simple. He felt that the dictum was not exact and scientific enough to provide the necessary proofs for the elements of Christian doctrine. What, for instance, was meant by "always"? Did it suppose the explicit presence of a doctrine at any time under consideration, and hence always? If so, the doctrines concerning the Blessed Virgin Mary could not easily have been shown to be the true doctrine of the original Church. Or what was meant by "everywhere"? Did it mean that every part of the Church had been infused with a given doctrine? [43]

From these suppositions, Newman developed the *Essay* into an elaborate and comprehensive work on the development of

---

[39] Louis Bouyer, *Newman: His Life and Spirituality* (New York: P. J. Kenedy & Sons, 1958), 249.

[40] John Henry Newman, *Essay on the Development of Christian Doctrine*, ed. J. M. Cameron (Middlesex, England: Penguin Books, 1974), 69–73.

[41] See Ian Ker, *John Henry Newman: A Biography* (Oxford University Press, 1988), 302.

[42] Newman, *An Essay on the Development*, 74.

[43] See Biemer, *Newman on Tradition*, 54–55.

Christian doctrine. As Günter Biemer succinctly summarized his conclusions:

> The relative insufficiency of St. Vincent's rule was, there-
> fore, the occasion for Newman to seek for more objective
> characteristics of Tradition, that is, of the true development
> of a system of ideas. And now he gives the seven criteria
> which were to become famous:
> 1. The Preservation of Type
> 2. The Continuity of Principle
> 3. The Power of Assimilation
> 4. Logical Sequence
> 5. Anticipation of the Future
> 6. Conservation Action upon the Past
> 7. Chronic Vigour.
> In the light of these criteria, and with their help, Newman
> demonstrates that the Catholic Church of the first, third
> and fourth, fifth and sixth centuries, corresponds in type—
> or, we could also say, in structure—to the present Church of
> Rome. Or he can show that the power to adapt and assimi-
> late, without detriment to the truth—a characteristic which
> puritanical and esoteric Christian circles have so often made
> a reproach—is a constant criterium of the Church of Jesus.
> ... The result of Newman's survey of the history of
> dogma in the Church's history as such was a fundamental
> and profound optimism with regard to the true doctrine and
> its preservation from corruption.[44]

With these conclusions developed in the *Essay*, Newman was in great confusion during the latter part of 1844. As he wrote in the *Apologia*—"I came to the resolutions of writing an Essay on Doctrinal Development; and then, if, at the end of it, my con-victions in favour of the Roman Church were not weaker, of taking the necessary steps for admission into her fold."[45] But the decision was to be an agonizing one as he indicated on 16 November 1844—"I am going through what must be gone through; and my trust only is that every day of pain is so much taken from the necessary draught which must be exhausted."[46]

---

[44] Ibid., 55–56.
[45] *Apologia*, 206.
[46] Ibid.

An interesting indication of how tumultuous those times must have been for Newman was a postscript that was included in an advertisement for the original 1845 edition of the *Essay*:

> Since the above was written, the author has joined the Catholic Church. It was his intention and wish to have carried his volume through the press before deciding finally on this step. But when he had got some way in the printing, he recognized in himself a conviction of the truth of the conclusions to which the discussion leads, so clear as to supersede further deliberation. Shortly afterwards circumstances gave him the opportunity of acting upon it, and he felt that he had no warrant for refusing to do so.[47]

The Conversion of John Henry Newman

Thus, with his heart and mind in such a state of turmoil, Newman attempted, for a time, to hold on to the resolution that he had made to wait until the *Essay* was published before making the final decision about leaving the Church of England. He struggled through the spring and summer of 1845. However, "he found those around him, whose simpler minds were strangers to his own resolve to resist the promptings of impulse for a fixed time, on the point of being received."[48]

> Ambrose St. John and Dalgairns were on a holiday and wrote that they had actually joined the Church of Rome. Henry Wilberforce, on the other hand, who still hoped against hope to keep Newman in the Church of England, wrote urging him against being received in Advent or at Christmas—hoping that delay might yet save him. Newman accepted this advice as an excuse to move not later, but earlier. Dalgairns had been on September 27 to Aston to be admitted into the Church by Father Dominic the Passionist. Father Dominic was to come to visit his convert at Littlemore on October 8 on his way to Belgium. Here was the occasion which Providence supplied. Here was the "kindly light" which relieved his uncertainty and marked out for him the immediate course.[49]

---

[47] Quoted in *An Essay on the Development*, 64.
[48] Wilfred Ward, *Life of . . . Newman*, 1:91–92.
[49] Ibid., 1:92.

These happenings seemed to be the impetus that Newman needed. On October 3, he wrote a letter to the Provost of Oriel in which he resigned his fellowship. On that same day he wrote to Pusey and indicated that anything could happen momentarily. On October 7, St. John returned to Littlemore, whereupon Newman wrote the following to Henry Wilberforce:

> Father Dominic the Passionist is passing this way, on his way from Aston in Staffordshire to Belgium, where a chapter of his Order (if it is an Order) is to be held at this time. He is to come to Littlemore for a night as a guest of one of us whom he has admitted at Aston. He does not know of my intentions, but I shall ask of him admission into the one true Fold of the Redeemer. I shall keep this back till after it is all over.
>
> I could have wished to delay till my book was actually out, but having all along gone so simply and entirely by my own reason, I was not sorry in this matter of time, at an inconvenience, to submit myself to what seemed an external call. Also I suppose the departure of others has had something to do with it, for when they went, it was as if I were losing my own bowels.[50]

There could be no doubt that Newman was distraught that his friends had left the Church of England for Rome, but Newman was also certain that God's Divine Providence, the "external call," had brought the "simple quaint man, an Italian," to the doors of Littlemore to convert him to Catholicism. The idea of having an Italian priest as the instrument of conversion seemed to appeal to Newman, but there were other advantages of this decision. "Newman was not in contact with any Catholic priest except Father Dominic and Father Charles Russell at Maynooth in Ireland—so the arrival of Father Dominic made reception easy without drawing a great deal of attention to what was happening—though of course the news spread like wildfire." [51]

Thus, on the evening of 9 October 1845, John Henry New-

---

[50] Newman, *Letters and Diaries*, 11:3.
[51] Father Gregory Winterton, "Don't Forget Blessed Dominic," in *Friends of Cardinal Newman Newsletter* (New Year, 2005), 10.

man became a Catholic. That same day and the next, Newman spent in correspondence with many friends—most of the letters were short and to the point, simple declarations of his intentions: "I am to be received into what I believe to be the one Church and the one Communion of Saints this evening, if it is so ordered. Father Dominic the Passionist is here, and I have begun my confession to him. I suppose two friends will be received with me." [52]

In a letter of October, 1845, Father Dominic Barberi recounted in detail the reception of John Henry Newman into the "one Church":

> And now I am going to give you a piece of news that will fill your heart with joy, and not yours only, but the heart of every good Catholic the world over. Already I had written you from Aston that on St. Michael's Day I had received the adjuration of Mr. John Dobree Dalgairns in our Chapel at Aston Hall, and with whom, as you knew, I have corresponded ever since my arrival in England. Well, when he learned that I was leaving for Belgium he wrote and asked me to call at Oxford on the way, telling me that I might have something to do there. In view of this invitation, I left Aston on the 8th, and reached Oxford at ten o'clock that night, soaked with rain. Hardly had I reached the inn, when I found Mr. Dalgairns waiting to take me out to Littlemore, the monastery established about three years back by Rev. John Henry Newman. There these Oxford men lead a penitential life much more severe than that usually led by Religious. We reached Littlemore about an hour before midnight, and I took up my position before the fire to dry myself. The door opened—and what a spectacle it was for me to see at my feet John Henry Newman begging me to hear his confession and admit him into the bosom of the Catholic Church! And there by the fire he began his general confession with extraordinary humility and devotion. In the morning, I betook myself to Oxford to say Mass in a Catholic Church there, and returned to Littlemore once more amid pouring rain. There I terminated Mr. Newman's confession, and then heard the confession of two other gentlemen who

---

[52] Newman, "To T. W. Allies," *Letters and Diaries*, 11:12.

were there, namely, Revs. Stanton and Bowles, both of them, like Newman, ministers of the Church of England. That same evening about six o'clock, I received the profession of Faith of all three, and gave them conditional baptism. On the following morning, Feast of St. Francis Borgia, I said Holy Mass for the first time in their private oratory. I had previously borrowed all that was necessary from a good priest of the neighbourhood. At the Mass, I gave Holy Communion to Mr. Newman and four other companions of his, formerly Protestants, and now most fervent Catholics. . . .

The following morning—i.e., on the eleventh—after I had said Mass again in the private Chapel at Littlemore, I came on to London, where I preached on Sunday last. Then I came on here to Tournai, which I reached safely last evening. . . .

These are the details of my Oxford visit. Those who know Mr. Newman and his companions will be in a position to judge and weigh the results of such an event. Newman has been up to now what I might term the Pope of the Protestants, their oracle, the soul of the Puseyite party, which is the most widely diffused in the Church of England and embraces all that is serious and devout in the Protestant Church. He is reputed to be the most learned ecclesiastic in England. In my judgement, he is one of the most humble and lovable men I have met in my life. Let us hope that the results of such conversions may be incalculable. All that I have suffered since I left Italy is well compensated by such a happy event as this. I pray that all good Religious everywhere may be spurred on to pray more fervently than ever for our most dear England!

Once she was the island of saints, and so may she be once again! This daughter of the Church, who for three centuries has strayed from the path, will surely return full of vigour to her mother the holy Catholic and apostolic Roman Church. So may it be![53]

How ironic it was that "the Pope of the Protestants" was converted by the little Italian priest. And the influence of Father Dominic was not to fade from the minds of his converts. "The neophytes henceforth followed the simple rule of life

---

[53] Father Dominic Barberi, quoted in Gwynn, *Dominic Barberi*, 138–140.

prescribed by Father Dominic. On Sunday, October 12, the little church of St. Clement's, Oxford, saw for the first time the group of Littlemore—St. John, Dalgairns, and Stanton—accompanying Newman to Mass." [54] On All Saints Day, Newman and his friends were confirmed by Bishop Wiseman in the Catholic seminary at Oscott, and together Newman and Wiseman began to formulate plans for the future of the men of Littlemore.

Later in November, Newman summarized these considerations:

> I had then a very satisfactory talk with Dr. Wiseman, as far as talks can be satisfactory. He distinctly stated that "he wished Old Oscott to be Littlemore continued"—his was "precisely his view." He wished laymen there—he wished anyone to be there who otherwise would have come to me. He wished it to be "a place of refuge." He agreed that we could not know our calling yet, and I believe I used, and he accepted, the word "provisional" as applied to our assemblage. What he wanted, he said, was this—a body of men educated above the common run—not for ordinary missionary purposes, but for extraordinary; principally for two objects—first to meet the growing Germanism and infidelity of the times by literature– next to be preachers, e.g., to conduct what has such great effect abroad but has never been attempted in England, series of sermons through Advent, Lent, etc.—and that not in one locality, but in Birmingham, "in London," or any where else. He would for our education, place one or two experienced priests at Old Oscott, not deep divines but accurate school divines, who would be able to teach us what we ought to know, etc., etc., to direct us, to conduct retreats, and to perform the Chapel service—and he would ordain at the end of one, two, or three years, according to the particular case. This was the sum of what he said—He added that he wished me to go to Rome, but not at once because I was just now useful to persons who were coming over—and he said that very likely he might be able to go with me. [55]

[54] Wilfred Ward, *Life of . . . Newman*, 1:95.
[55] Newman, "To James Hope," *Letters and Diaries*, 11:47–48.

For Newman, therefore, there was much that had been abandoned, and there was much that needed to be done. He had given up his denominational affiliation, his ministry, and the respect of many of his family and friends. But the ultimate steps had been taken. Newman had completed and had published his *Essay on the Development of Christian Doctrine*, which defined the static and dynamic aspects of Christian Tradition. He had been converted by Father Dominic Barberi, who would become for Newman the prototype of a humble, totally altruistic Catholic priest, and, in addition, Barberi had given him his first true religious instruction as a Catholic.

However, from that point on, John Henry Newman was taking those elements that he had already acknowledged and was searching for his own identity within that Roman Catholic world. He realized that he needed to leave the security of his life at Littlemore for the uncertainty of the new demands of Oscott. Further, he knew that there were many questions that were still unanswered—questions about a future community for his group and about the possibility of Catholic priesthood for some or all of its members. But the one most significant realization was that he needed to go to Rome, to the cradle of Catholicism, to answer some of these questions. Eventually, it would be in Rome that Newman would meet other Italians, who would help him define more clearly his future life as a Catholic.

V

THE TRADITION OF CATHOLIC PRIESTHOOD

Newman's Second Trip to Italy (1846)

The effects of John Henry Newman's conversion to Catholicism were to reverberate throughout England and, indeed, throughout the Christian world. In the next few years, several hundred other men from the educated echelon of English society followed Newman's example and abandoned the Anglican Church to become Catholics. Dean Church[1] explained that "through the autumn and the next year, friends whose names and forms were familiar in Oxford, one by one disappeared and were lost to it. Fellowships, livings, curacies, intended careers were given up. . . . A considerable portion of English society learned what it was to be novices in a religious system, hitherto not only alien and unknown, but dreaded, or else to have lost friends and relatives, who were suddenly transformed into severe and uncompromising opponents."[2]

Newman was also beginning a new life in a new world. When he went from Littlemore to Oscott at the end of November, he had some unusual experiences—some quite distressing and others even somewhat amusing. But in all instances, he was being drawn closer to Catholicism and its traditions. At that point, he seemed reluctant to make any permanent decisions about the future. He was concerned that Bishop Wiseman was moving too quickly for him. As he wrote to the Bishop—"I see

---

[1] Richard William Church met Newman in 1836 and was elected a Fellow of Oriel in 1838. Although Newman wrote in 1845 that Church was one of the few people who still spoke to him after the conversion, their friendship was soon suspended and not renewed until 1865 (*Letters and Diaries*, 11:336).

[2] R. W. Church, in Charles Stephen Dessain, *John Henry Newman* (Stanford, Calif.: Stanford University Press, 1971), 89.

the extreme advantages of being connected with your Lordship and Oscott; . . . but I am afraid of a step which implicates others besides myself, and not only those who are now with me, but who may wish to be, nay some who are as yet members of the Anglican Church. They are so different from each other, and their calling so uncertain that I should be very loath to do anything to commit them absolutely to a particular course or a particular place, any more than myself. . . ." [3]

In addition to Bishop Wiseman, Frederick Faber was one of the few who approved of Newman's conversion, and he was excitedly spurring Newman onward to the "Roman" way of life:[4]

> He [Faber] had been living an increasingly Roman, not to say Italian, life in his parish at Elton. On a visit to Rome, he had picked up many Catholic devotions, which he practiced before leaving the Anglican Church, shocking the fox-hunting gentry with his goings on. He was just over thirty, about the same age as Ambrose St. John. At Oxford, he had been known as a poet, and in early portraits he looked the part, with the dark locks of poets of the Romantic period, and large lustrous eyes. An enthusiast, he charmed a great many people, and so fascinated his simple parishioners that there were dramatic scenes when he left, sobs and tears. He took with him a band of country youths, some hardly more than boys, who had been confessing to him, praying, and taking the discipline. At present, he was living with them in Birmingham, in a house which, inside, was intended to make them feel they were in Italy, so full of pictures, statues and lights as to astonish some of the sturdy English Catholics who called. Faber was known as Brother Wilfred, and his young men were known as Wilfridians, though he called them Brothers of the Will of God. Father Dominic, shrewd holy man, called them "Brothers of the Will of Faber." It was possibly Faber's excited conversation as well as the gas that made Newman's head ache. [Newman had commented

[3] Newman, "To Bishop Wiseman," *Letters and Diaries*, 11:53–54.

[4] Frederick William Faber: In 1848, he and his "Wilfridians" joined the English Oratory; and, when the London Oratory was founded the following year, Newman put Faber in charge. When it became independent, Faber was its Superior until his death (*Letters and Diaries*, 11:339–340).

that being too much in the company of Faber made his head hurt.] [5]

In the meantime, Father Dominic was writing articles about Newman and his conversion which were being published throughout England. Newman described his feelings to St. John: "I declare I doubt whether I shall have courage to look into F. Dominic's Epistle. One must bear the infliction as one does a stomach ache; with the feeling that grumbling does no good." [6] Obviously, Faber and Barberi were demonstrating too much Italian enthusiasm too soon for the normally staid and demure Dr. Newman, who was once again very happy to escape back to the peacefulness of Littlemore.

However, the influence of those two Catholics was not in vain, and in a few months Newman himself caught the "Roman fever." From that time forward, Newman seemed to take the lead, and he gradually began to make his own plans for the future. He finally accepted Bishop Wiseman's offer to spend some time at Oscott, and the parting from Littlemore became imminent. Although he still bemoaned the loss of so many dear ones, he started to embrace Catholic ideas and traditions:

> I am now engaged in looking over, sorting, burning my papers and letters, and have had pangs and uttered deep sighs, such as I have not at all yet (though I used before) since my reception into the Church. So many dead, so many separated. My mother gone; my sisters nothing to me, or rather foreign to me; of my greatest friends Froude, Wood, Bowden taken away, all of whom would now be, or be coming, on my side. Other dear friends who *are* preserved in life *not* moving with me. . . . Of my friends of a dozen years ago, whom have I now? And what did I know of my present friends a dozen years ago? Why, they were at School, or they were freshmen looking up to me, if they knew my name, as some immense and unapproachable don; and now they know nothing, can know nothing of my earlier life; things

[5] Meriol Trevor, *Newman: The Pillar of the Cloud* (Garden City, N.Y.: Doubleday & Co., 1962), 368.
[6] Newman, "To Ambrose St. John," *Letters and Diaries*, 11:45.

which to me are as yesterday are to them as dreams of the past; they do not know the names, the state of things, the occurrences, they have not the associations, which are part of my own world, in which I live. And yet I am very happy with them, and can truly say with St. Paul "I have all and abound"—and moreover, I have with them, what I never can have had with others. Catholic hopes and beliefs— Catholic objects.[7]

With his decision to embrace the Catholic Faith, John Henry Newman left behind all that had been of importance to him—his Anglican life, his family, his position, and his friends. What his letters indicated, however, despite such a loss of things beloved, he had gained much more than could ever be measured. For now, he had a Faith and a Tradition that could be traced back to St. Paul, and he had friends with whom he could truly share these beliefs. Further, Newman mentioned often in his writings that he had learned many of the daily Catholic practices from Father Dominic Barberi, who was at this point his mentor in the Faith. In fact, Newman seemed to be very comfortable following what he had learned from Liguori and Barberi and incorporating their teachings into his new existence as a Catholic. They had given him a strong foundation upon which to build and expand his faith.

One by one, Newman's friends left Littlemore to prepare their new residences at Oscott. Newman himself arrived there late in February of 1846. Newman was greeted by some of the more influential Catholics, including George Talbot, who would later become an intimate of Blessed Pope Pius IX, and Henry Formby, another enthusiastic priest who was eager to befriend Newman. On the following day, Newman and St. John spent the afternoon visiting with Bishop Wiseman. "Soon, however, the regular life of Littlemore was resumed, though the rules given by Father Dominic gave place to fresh ones drawn up by Bishop Wiseman. The little community consisted of eight

---

[7] Newman, "To Miss M. R. Giberne," *Letters and Diaries*, 11:101.

persons—Newman, St. John, Stanton, J. B. Morris, Formby, Walker, Christie, and Penny." [8]

Both Bishop Wiseman and Spencer Northcote [9] encouraged Newman to take advantage of the attention he was getting because of the *Essay on Development* and his conversion and to write an account of his reasons for becoming a Catholic. Newman declined because he felt that he could never adequately define all of the influences that had caused the growth of his mind and heart, nor could he explicate fully the role that Divine Providence was now playing in his life:

> I do not know how to do justice to my reasons for becoming a Catholic in ever so many words—but if I attempted to do so in few, and that in print, I should wantonly expose myself and my cause to the hasty and prejudiced criticisms of opponents. This I will not do. People shall not say, "We have now got his reasons, and know their worth." No, you have not got them, you cannot get them, except at the cost of some portion of the trouble I have been at myself. You cannot buy them for a crown piece—You cannot take them in your hand at your will, and toss them about. You must consent to think—and you must exercise such resignation to the Divine Hand which leads you, as to follow it any whither. I am not assuming that my reasons are sufficient or unanswerable, when I say this—but describing the way in which alone our intellect can be successfully exercised on the great subject in question, if the intellect is to be the instrument of conversion. Moral proofs are grown into, not learnt by heart. [10]

In the months that followed, Newman put aside all controversial writing and set himself to learn the ways and traditions of his new religious home and to help his little community at Maryvale [11] to prepare for their ministry. They seemed to be

[8] Wilfred Ward, *The Life of John Henry Cardinal Newman* (London: Longmans, Green, and Co., 1912), 1:120.

[9] James Spencer Northcote: Oxford scholar who was influenced by Newman and became a Catholic in 1846. He traveled in Italy and became an authority on Christian antiquities. After his wife's death in 1853, he studied for the priesthood under Newman at Birmingham (*Letters and Diaries*, 11:349–350).

[10] Newman, "To J. Spencer Northcote," *Letters and Diaries*, 11:110.

[11] Maryvale was the new name given to Oscott by Newman, possibly in deference to what he had learned from the writings of St. Alfonsus Liguori.

considering two alternate plans for the future. Father Dominic Barberi had suggested that Newman and his friends be preachers, missionaries, and martyrs, while Bishop Wiseman had the idea that they should use their special gifts in contending with modern infidelity by founding a school of divinity. "The 'Friars preachers' founded by St. Dominic and made illustrious in the schools by St. Thomas Aquinas were by their history marked out for such a work, and the suggestion was discussed that Newman and his friends should become Dominicans." [12]

With all of these ideas swirling about, Newman and Wiseman decided that Newman should go in the summer to Rome to the College of Propaganda, which was the seminary for students from mission countries. He had told Wiseman that he wanted a regular education in a place where he would be under obedience and discipline for a time. The College was known to be a very strict school, and Newman would be like a child once again, learning his religion. [13] Newman had utilized the foundations of Catholic Tradition that he learned from Liguori and Barberi and was now ready to begin a more formal education in Catholic theology.

Even though Newman knew that only in Italy could he obtain the training that he needed, the trip itself would not be an easy one for him. He mentioned several times that the voyage would be a very great trial to him at his time of life (he was now forty-five years old) and with his stationary habits. However, he realized that beyond the clerical and spiritual training that he would get in Italy, he needed the exposure to the religious orders that were based there in order to determine definitely his future mission in England:

> The question is whether I could get authority and sanction at Rome to form a school of theology, the future form of which would be left to the future. But what would the Jesuits say to it, with whom I should be so much thrown at Propa-

[12] Wilfred Ward, *Life of . . . Newman*, 1:124.
[13] See Ian Ker, *John Henry Newman: A Biography* (Oxford University Press, 1988), 321.

ganda? Then it strikes me on the other hand what, if when I get among them, I am persuaded to *be* a Jesuit with this theological prospect—but, if so, what will Dr. Wiseman say to it, in whose house we and our library are? Then you see, I see nothing except that the notion of a theological school is a great idea—and natural, not only from our hitherto line of reading, but because the Rosminians (whom I cannot quite like) are fast spreading themselves, as givers of retreats and missions, all over England. I have been thinking lately of an institution having the express object of propagating the faith (the Dominican object) and opposing heresy—whether by teaching, preaching, controversy, catechizing, etc., etc. . . . Else, I sketched out the faint outlines of a community under the patronage of St. Mary *quae sola interemisti*, etc., with the object of 1st adoring 2nd defending the *Mysteries* of Faith.[14]

Only in Italy could these questions be answered for Newman.

Newman decided that he would like Ambrose St. John to accompany him during his stay in Rome, and the two departed from Brighton, England, for France on 8 September 1846. Unlike his first trip to Italy when he felt strange and alienated in this totally Catholic environment, Newman now looked upon Italy as the embodiment of Catholic Tradition. As Wilfred Ward said in 1912, "Newman approached . . . Catholic Italy in the spirit which I have already noted as marking the first years of his life in his new Communion. The halo of 'the blessed vision of peace,' of which he speaks at the end of the *Essay on Development*, bathed in its light all manifestations of Catholic life, feeling, and devotion. Some of his letters are like those of a man in love . . . for whom every look and action of the woman he loves is transfigured."[15]

This nascent love of Catholicism and its traditions helped Newman to look much more kindly upon Italy than he had as a visitor in 1833. When he and St. John reached Milan on September 20, Newman was delighted with the church attached to the priests' house where they were staying. "I fear I like that style of architecture more than some of our Oscott and Birmingham

[14] Newman, "To J. D. Dalgairns," *Letters and Diaries*, 11:196.
[15] Wilfred Ward, *Life of . . . Newman*, 1:133.

friends would approve. The brightness, grace, and simplicity of
the classical style seem more to befit the notion of St. Mary or St.
Gabriel than any thing in Gothic." In addition to preferring the
Italian architecture over the English, Newman was utterly enthralled with the city of Milan and its illustrious history. As he
explained—"This is a most wonderful place—to me more striking than Rome. To be sure, I was not a Catholic when there—
but then Milan presents more associations with the history,
which is familiar to me, than Rome. Here were St. Ambrose, St.
Augustine, St. Monica, St. Athanasius, etc." [16]

But, most of all, in Italy Newman found what he felt was a
real Catholic religion practiced in a real Catholic country by
real Catholic people:

> It is really most wonderful to see this Divine Presence look-
> ing out almost into the open streets from the various
> churches, so that at St. Laurence's we saw the people take off
> their hats from the other side of the street as they passed
> along; no one to guard it, but perhaps an old woman who
> sits at work before the church door, or has some wares to
> sell. . . .
>
> I have said not a word about that overpowering place, the
> Duomo. . . . And, as I have said for months past that I never
> knew what worship was, as an objective fact, till I entered
> the Catholic Church, and was partaker in its offices of devo-
> tion, so now I say the same on the view of its cathedral
> assemblages. . . . A Catholic cathedral is a sort of world,
> every one going about his own business, but that business a
> religious one; groups of worshippers, and solitary ones—
> kneeling, standing—some at shrines, some at altars—hear-
> ing Mass and communicating—currents of worshipers inter-
> cepting and passing by each other—altar after altar lit up for
> worship, like stars in the firmament—or the bell giving no-
> tice of what is going on in parts you do not see—and all the
> while the canons in the choir going through matins and
> lauds, and at the end of it the incense rolling up from the
> high altar, and all this in one of the most wonderful buildings
> in the world and every day—lastly, all of this without any

[16] Newman, "To W. G. Penny," *Letters and Diaries*, 11:249.

show or effort, but what every one is used to—every one at
his own work, and leaving every one else to his.[17]

Feeling as if in Milan they had finally found Catholic examples to follow, Newman and St. John, likewise, went about
their "own work." They received several of their English
friends, and on September 29 they began in earnest to study the
language of Italy. In addition, Italian manners and Italian compliments were learned, and to Newman's great delight, St. John
parted from an Italian friend, whom they expected to see again
in Rome the following January, expressing in confident Italian
a strong hope that they would shortly meet again "in hell"—for
he pronounced "inverno" (winter) as it were "inferno." Newman's diary was almost without entries during that entire visit,
since the time was being spent in visiting all of the interesting
sights of Milan.[18] As he said to Dalgairns towards the end of the
visit—"We have been so happy here for a month or five weeks,
I quite dread the moving again." [19]

On October 21, Newman and St. John paid their last visit to
the churches of Milan, and on the morning of the 23rd, they left
for Rome. The day after their arrival, they went straight to St.
Peter's and by a fortunate coincidence found the Pope himself
(Giovanni Ferretti—Pius IX) saying Mass. That same day they
paid visits to Cardinal Fransoni, the prefect of the College of
Propaganda (Collegio di Propaganda Fide) and to Monsignor
Brunelli, secretary of the College, both of whom would soon
become their friends. Although they were making Italian
friends in high places, they spent their time at the Collegio as
students who were preparing themselves for ordination to the
priesthood. They were "middle-aged men among a multitude
of young seminarians, some of them mere boys." [20] But they
knew what their goals were, and by November Newman's Italian was good enough (although he always was modest about his
language ability) to enable him to write the following to Father

[17] Newman "To Henry Wilberforce," *Letters and Diaries*, 11:252–253.
[18] See Wilfred Ward, *Life of . . . Newman*, 1:142.
[19] Newman, "To J. D. Dalgairns," *Letters and Diaries*, 11:263.
[20] John Moody, *John Henry Newman* (New York: Sheed & Ward, 1945), 152.

Ghianda who was the Abbot of the College: "At the present moment we are so preoccupied with the study of theology and Latin, that we have little time to study Italian, even though it is always spoken here. This explains my style, of which I am much ashamed . . . . we are waiting while to meet the Pope in little while." [21]

The year in Italy would be very momentous for Newman, and the two highlights were meeting the Pope and his ordination to the priesthood. Having come from an anti-papal background, Newman was surprisingly impressed with Pius IX. "He is a young hale-looking man, though past 50—with a most unaffected familiar manner. He had several times asked about me, only that very morning, (but it did not depend on me, but on the people here)—and was very kind, I should say affectionate, were it a private person. He gave me a very handsome oil painting of the Blessed Virgin as the Mater Dolorosa. It was quite a private visit; we were in the same dress as which we walk the streets in, or sit at home." [22]

In addition to making friends with Italian dignitaries, Newman still found time for other work. As Moody explained in his biography:

> But even in Rome, busy as he was with matters connected with his preparation for the priesthood, planning his Oratory and making contacts with many people, he was filling his leisure moments with his pen. This was never idle; that "passion for scribbling" which he says possessed him in his boyhood days was as potent as ever. And although before he left for Rome he had declined to write anything bearing on his conversion, he was inspired, while viewing the Roman scene. . . to turn his thoughts to the writing of a book. The result was *Loss and Gain*, which, if not completed in Rome, must have been planned and outlined there. It appeared shortly after his return home and achieved a wide circulation. It was immediately accepted as Newman's own story, or at least as basically autobiographical, which indeed it was.

[21] Newman, "To Abbate Ghianda," *Letters and Diaries*, 11:78.
[22] Newman, "To Mrs. John Mozley," *Letters and Diaries*, 11:282–283.

Bishop Wiseman, whom Newman had repulsed at Oscott for urging him to write his conversion story, must now have indulged in a quiet chuckle.[23]

There could be no question that *Loss and Gain*, Newman's first work as a Catholic, could not have been written if he had not been so deeply affected by Italy and the Italians. There were scenes in the book that could only have been inspired by what he saw during his second visit. "That vivid description of the Mass and its significance was surely conceived by Newman while in Rome, where, for the first time, in his rounds of the great Roman churches, he absorbed atmosphere and scenes which he never could have absorbed at home."[24]

Further, Newman now began to see in Italy the evidence that Revelation was not a simple set of facts and propositions which could be mastered by reason alone. He was entranced with the way in which the Italians threw themselves heart and soul into their religious beliefs. He told Wilberforce: "One thing has struck me here and everywhere—the monstrous absurdity of supposing that the Catholic priests are not most absolute and utter believers in the divinity of their own system. They are believers so as to be bigots—their fault is that they generally cannot conceive how educated Englishmen can be Anglicans with a good conscience—but they have a profound confidence in the truth of Catholicism."[25]

Newman was amazed to see the innate respect that Italians had for their Church and their religion, and he transferred those feelings to his main character in *Loss and Gain*, Charles Reding: "A cloud of incense was rising on high; the people suddenly all bowed low; what could it mean? The truth flashed on him, fearfully yet sweetly; it was the Blessed Sacrament—it was the Lord Incarnate Who was on the altar, Who had come to visit and to bless His people. It was the Great Presence, which makes a Catholic church different from every other place in the

[23] Moody, *John Henry Newman*, 157.
[24] Ibid., 160.
[25] Newman, "To Henry Wilburforce," *Letters and Diaries*, 11:295.

world; which makes it as no other place can be, holy." [26] Running throughout the novel is a sense of reality and unreality. Whatever its alleged superstitions, Roman Catholicism was real. Conversely, whatever high Anglicans may have believed or said, the Church of England was a "Protestant reality" but "a Catholic sham." [27]

Finally, *Loss and Gain* could not, also, have been written without the presence of Father Dominic Barberi in Newman's life. The conversion of Charles Reding to Catholicism is eerily reminiscent of Newman's own conversion just a year before, and Father Dominic was surely the model for the Passionist priest:

> At the time of our narrative, Father Domenico de Matre Dei had become familiar with England; he had had many anxieties here, first from want of funds, then still more from want of men. . . . And now the reader knows much more about the Passionists than did Reding at the time that he made his way to their monastery.
>
> . . . A very few words will conduct us to the end of our history. It was Sunday morning about seven o'clock, and Charles had been admitted into the communion of the Catholic Church about an hour since. He was still kneeling in the church of the Passionists before the tabernacle, in the possession of a deep peace and serenity of mind, which he had not thought possible on earth. It was more like the stillness which almost sensibly affects the ears, when a bell which had long been tolling stops, or when a vessel, after much tossing at sea, finds itself in harbor.[28]

Newman even finished this work with the image of a tossing vessel at sea, possibly in memory of his trip home from Palermo when he wrote "Lead, Kindly Light."

However, the main focus of this year in Italy was priesthood preparation for Newman and for St. John. At last, on 26 May 1847, St. Philip's Day, both were ordained subdeacons by Cardinal Fransoni in his private chapel. On the following Saturday,

[26] Newman, *Loss and Gain* (Boston: Patrick Donahoe, 1854), 250.

[27] Ian Ker, *John Henry Newman*, 333.

[28] Newman, *Loss and Gain*, 248–251.

they were made deacons at St. John Lateran, and on Trinity Sunday, June 1, they were ordained to the priesthood by Cardinal Fransoni in the church at Propaganda. In a small chapel there, Newman said his first Mass on the following Thursday which was the Feast of Corpus Christi. "He said nothing of these events in his letters, simply recording them in his diary." [29] Yet when he wrote to Pope Pius IX just three weeks after his ordination, he proudly called himself in Italian, "il sacerdote Giovanni Maria Newman [the priest, John Mary Newman]." [30]

Newman and the Novelist Alessandro Manzoni

Padre Giovanni Maria Neandri was now a Catholic priest, and he would need to find a model for the kind of priest that he wanted to be and the form of ministry in which he and his fellow converts would engage. The search for Catholic priests whom he could admire had started earlier in his career. In 1837, he wrote to his sister that he had read a book that she had mentioned and that he had been quite enthralled with its spirituality: "I have lately been reading a novel you spoke of, *I Promessi Sposi*, and am quite delighted with it. It has not the vigor or richness of Walter Scott, but it seems to me full of nature, and displays a depth of religious feeling, which never approaches W. S.'s compositions, beautiful as they are. It is most inspiring—it quite transported me in parts." [31]

In fact, Newman was so taken with *I Promessi Sposi* (*The Betrothed*), by Alessandro Manzoni, that later that year he suggested that his friend Keble should write a review of the novel. Newman felt that he and his fellow Englishmen knew so little about the actual workings of Catholicism that such a review would enlighten them—"As to Romanism, we all know but a little—but still the contrast with our own way of going on is so striking that a person may know much negatively." [32] Unfortunately, Keble did

---

[29] Trevor, 417.
[30] Newman, "To Pope Pius IX," *Letters and Diaries*, 12:87.
[31] Newman, "To Mrs. John Mozley," *Letters and Diaries*, 6:150.
[32] Newman, "To John Keble," *Letters and Diaries*, 6:328.

not feel up to the task because he, also, had had no practical experience with the "Roman" system, and the review was never done.

But Newman did not lose interest in Manzoni and *I Promessi Sposi*, and he would mention them time and again. In late 1839, when he was in despair over the situation for priests in England, he turned to Manzoni and his character of Fra Cristoforo. Newman explained to his friend Frederic Rogers that this monk, an Italian and a Catholic, was a true example of how a priest of God should live his life.

> Your account of your priest is amusing. *Can* the R. C.'s have any tender feeling towards Anglicanism? Who among us ever showed them any kindness? Are we not pets of a State which made it a felony to celebrate Mass even, I believe, in private, a law which Ward declares remained in existence till 1780? *What* are the R. C.'s to admire in us? Our married bishops or our dissenting brethren? I cannot deny that my heart is with neither of these—where it is 'tis more difficult to say, but I saw yesterday (by chance in a letter which I had sent home from the Continent,) that I then considered I had left "half of it at Rome." What a sad case of divided allegiance—with one's duty one way, and one's love another—still let it be.
>
> You see, if things were to come to the worst, I should turn Brother of Charity in London—an object which, *quite* independently of any such perplexities, is growing on me, and peradventure, will some day be accomplished, if other things do not impede me. The Capuchin in the *Promessi Sposi* has struck in my heart like a dart. I have never got over him. Only I think it would be, in sober seriousness, far too great an honour for such as me to have such a post, being little worthy or fit for it.[33]

Newman was not alone with these feelings, and his biographer Wilfred Ward mentioned that as time went by and more Englishmen read Manzoni, they likewise were impressed with the Catholicism depicted in the novel. Even Thomas Macaulay,

---

[33] Newman, "To Frederic Rogers," *Letters and Diaries*, 7:151.

the English essayist who was known for his calm rationalism, was moved to tears upon finishing Manzoni's novel. Macaulay stated, "If the Church of Rome really were what Manzoni represents her to be, I should be tempted to follow Newman's example." [34]

Considering the background of Alessandro Manzoni, it was surprising that he could have written a novel that would have spiritually influenced John Henry Newman and his contemporaries. Manzoni was born in 1785 on his father's estate near Lake Como, Italy. From the age of five, he was sent to boarding school where his mother never visited him. In fact, a few years later, she left his father to live in Paris with a wealthy Italian liberal. During those years that he was alone, Manzoni subscribed to the ideals of the French Revolution, and, in 1801, he wrote a poem which expressed harsh anti-Christian views. In 1805, Manzoni decided to live with his mother in Paris where he met a Swiss-Protestant woman named Henriette Blondel, whom he married in 1808. [35]

The marriage was a very happy one, except for a few tensions over religion which were resolved when both Manzoni and his wife became practicing Catholics. In 1810 they moved their family to Milan where Alessandro wrote a series of odes on religious subjects and several historical plays. He began work on *I Promessi Sposi* in 1821 and first published it in 1827. The novel was an instant success and ran to nine editions in four years. [36] There must have been, also, rapid translations, because Newman read the book barely ten years later at the suggestion of his sister.

After rewriting the book completely for a definitive edition which appeared in 1840, Manzoni seemed to lose enthusiasm for the creative aspects of his life. "He lived another thirty-three years, but they were not particularly happy ones. He had long suffered from a nervous disorder, which now grew worse.

[34] Wilfred Ward, *Life of . . . Newman*, 1:142.
[35] Bruce Penman, in Alessandro Manzoni, *The Betrothed* (*I Promessi Sposi*), ed. and trans. Bruce Penman (London: Penguin Books, 1972), 1.
[36] Ibid.

Henriette had died in 1833, his second wife also died many years before him, and only two of his nine children survived him. When he died in 1873, he was given a state funeral, and Verdi wrote his famous *Requiem* for the first anniversary of Manzoni's death." [37]

Millions of people the world over, including Newman and Macaulay, have been intrigued and inspired by *I Promessi Sposi,* which is set in turbulent seventeenth-century Italy. The story is an exciting one:

> Reflecting Manzoni's preoccupation with the suffering that is caused by tyranny in any form, the plot is thick with noblemen who use their power to flout law and justice, wreaking havoc in the lives of those who are too weak or too poor to protect themselves. At the centre of this turmoil are Renzo and Lucia, two lovers from a village near Lecco, who are forced to flee from the villainous Don Rodrigo. They are separated and each faces many dangers—violent riots, famine and plague—until they are united again. They also encounter a variety of people on their adventures: the Nun of Monza, whose strange manner hides a disturbing tale; Father Cristoforo, a man with a violent past and a passion for justice; and the Unnamed, the supreme tyrant. [38]

But Manzoni did not intend his novel to be merely an exciting saga. In *I Promessi Sposi,* he wanted to give the quintessential history of Catholic Italy in a form that most Italians could appreciate and understand. As the critic Bernard Wall has described its significance:

> The *Promessi Sposi* is accepted almost unanimously by Italian critics as the greatest novel in Italian literature, and it occupies a place more important than that in Italian life. It is not a book that interests only an *elite* of readers; it is essentially a *popular* book. People who otherwise read very little know the story of Renzo and Lucia almost by heart as they know the librettos of Verdi's operas. Characters such as Don Abbondio and Perpetua and the Conte Zio have become proverbial in the language—they are a part of Italian life as Don

[37] Ibid.
[38] Ibid.

Quixote and Sancho are a part of Spanish life. Italians see in *I Promessi Sposi* a mirror of their national character. To know Italy, we must appreciate Manzoni, but to appreciate Manzoni, I sometimes feel, we must know Italy, and I am not sure of the way out of this vicious circle.[39]

When Newman first read *I Promessi Sposi*, he certainly did not know Italy well, and, aside from his illness in Sicily, he had had very little experience of the Italian people. And, yet, the character of Fra Cristoforo moved him deeply. There were several aspects of the Catholic friar which certainly could have appealed to the young Anglican priest—Cristoforo was a Capuchin who had resurrected himself from an earlier dissipated existence to live a life of total devotion to God and His people. The introverted Newman probably romanticized the Italian Capuchins "for they owned nothing, wore a dress more strikingly different from other men than the other orders, made a more open profession of humility, and in all these ways exposed themselves more openly to both the veneration and the vilification which such things attract from men of various dispositions and various opinions."[40]

In addition, there was something so personally compelling about the manner in which Manzoni described the transformation of a "cocky young aristocrat named Lodovico who killed a man in a duel to settle the vain question of a right-of-way by a stone wall"[41] into the very complex and saintly Fra Cristoforo:

> We do not propose to record the detail of his monastic life; we will merely say that his two official duties were those of preaching and of tending the dying, which he carried out willingly and conscientiously, but that he never missed a chance of performing two other duties, which he had set himself—the composing of quarrels and the protection of the oppressed. Unknown to Father Cristoforo, an old habit had, to some extent, found its way back into his heart, together with a small remnant of his old combative spirit, which neither humiliation nor fasting had wholly been

---

[39] Bernard Wall, *Alessandro Manzoni* (New Haven: Yale University Press, 1954), 50.
[40] Manzoni, *The Betrothed*, trans. Bruce Penman, 73.
[41] Gian Piero Barricelli, *Alessandro Manzoni* (Boston: Twayne Publishers, 1976), 127.

able to extinguish. His language was generally humble and measured; but in any question of injury to justice or truth, the man would suddenly be animated by all his original fiery vigour, which, reinforced and subtly modified by the solemn emphasis he had learned in the pulpit, gave a singular character to his speech. Not only his face, but his whole manner, showed evidence of a long struggle between a passionate, touchy nature and a strong will, in which the will generally prevailed, remained permanently on guard, and drew its guidance from the highest motives and most lofty inspiration. . . .

If Father Cristoforo had received an appeal for help from some poor girl he had never met, who was in the same trouble as Lucia, he would have answered her call at once. He did so the more readily for Lucia, because he knew and admired her sweet and innocent nature, and because he was already deeply concerned about the danger in which she stood, and filled with holy indignation at the ignoble persecution she was suffering. Besides this, he had given her advice—the advice to say nothing and hush the matter up as the lesser of two evils—and now he was afraid that his counsels had produced some ill effect. So he felt not only the anxiety of Christian love, which was part of his nature, but that special self-questioning anguish which often troubles good men.[42]

Manzoni had created *I Promessi Sposi* and Fra Cristoforo in a manner that followed the Catholic tradition of narrating and revering the lives of the saints. He had the power of imposing a "story," a "myth" in the most powerful, archetypal sense, over the frailty of mere history. Manzoni insisted that the "bella storia" should be told and not discarded so that both the power of good and of evil in human existence could be revealed. The uncertainty of recovering the "truth" of history took nothing from the power and the truth of the "story." Manzoni illuminated not only *ciò che è* (things as they are) but also *ciò che può e dovrebbe essere* (things as they can and should be). [43]

[42] Manzoni, *The Betrothed*, trans. Bruce Penman, 90–91.
[43] Clarence G. Godt, *The Mobile Spectacle: Variable Perspective in Manzoni's* I Promessi Sposi (New York: Peter Lang, 1998), 154–155.

Thus, Newman would have been drawn to Fra Cristoforo as he had been drawn to individual portraits in the *Lives of the Saints*. These were the people who, with humility and charity, had given their entire beings to the service of God, and, despite the baseness of human existence, they showed how beautiful and rewarding a Christian life could be. By the late 1830s, Newman was very disillusioned with the compromises he had had to make as an Anglican priest, and the romanticism of Cristoforo's life must have been very appealing.

Although Newman never wrote a complete essay on Catholic priesthood, he did indicate in some of his works that the manner in which Cristoforo served was the ideal for his concept of Christian service, even though "it would be, in sober seriousness, far too great an honour for such as me to have such a post, being little worthy or fit for it." [44] Manzoni portrayed Cristoforo as the faithful and loyal priest—*il cavaliere di Cristo* (the knight of Christ). The Capuchin's message was one of devotion to God and His people: "I speak both for myself and for all my companions, who, without any merit of our own, have been chosen for the high honour of serving Christ by serving you, when I beg your forgiveness most humbly if we have failed in so great a mission." [45] Newman's own humility was a reflection of the humility expressed by Fra Cristoforo in his sermon to the Italian people.

Similarly, when Newman wrote about faithfulness, he echoed the type of faithfulness that Manzoni had embodied in the character of the priest:

> The word *faithfulness* means loyalty to a superior, or exactness in fulfilling an engagement. . . . And so, His true saints and servants have the special title of "faithful," as being true to Him as He is to them; as being simply obedient to His will, zealous for His honour, observant of the sacred interests which He has committed to their keeping. Thus Abraham is called The Faithful; Moses is declared to be faithful in all his house; David, on this account, is called the "man after God's

[44] Newman, *Letters and Diaries*, 7:151.
[45] Manzoni, *The Betrothed*, trans. Bruce Penman, 667.

own heart;" St. Paul returns thanks that "God accounted him faithful;" and, at the last day, God will say to all those who have well employed their talents, "Well done, good and faithful servant." [46]

Fra Cristoforo was faithful to the end, as he died of the plague while ministering to the stricken in the Lazzaretto.

Because Newman had felt such an immediate attraction to Manzoni and his character of the good Catholic priest, Newman was most anxious to meet the Italian novelist during his time in Italy while studying for the priesthood. In fact, when he was planning for the trip in August of 1846, he mentioned in a letter to Edward Badeley, "I propose going to Manzoni." [47] And, again, in a letter to T. F. Knox, he said, "We are somewhat anxious. St. John and I go first to Paris—then to Dalgairns at Langres—then to Milan where I wish to see Manzoni." [48] But, much to Newman's regret, the meeting never took place, and in an October letter to Dalgairns from Milan, he said, "We have missed Manzoni—but been lionized almost daily by his chaplain, Ghianda, whom we like very much indeed. He speaks Latin like a *native*, though he had given it up in his late conversations with us." [49]

Further, Newman received some figs from Ghianda, who said that they had come from Manzoni's favorite fig tree. In appreciation, Newman wrote in Italian to Ghianda expressing great respect and a hope of some day meeting Manzoni: " May Your Reverence be willing to accept my sentiments of great esteem, and my hope to see you, with which I have the honor of calling myself your most devoted servant." [50] There is evidence that the respect was mutual for, on 5 December 1846, "Ghianda sent a message from Manzoni of great regret at having missed Newman in Milan." [51]

[46] John Henry Newman, *Prayers, Verses, and Devotions* (San Francisco: Ignatius Press, 1989), 176–177.
[47] Newman, "To Edward Badeley," *Letters and Diaries*, 11:219.
[48] Newman, "To T. F. Knox," *Letters and Diaries*, 11:226.
[49] Newman, "To J. D. Dalgairns," *Letters and Diaries*, 11:262.
[50] Newman, "To Abbate Ghianda," *Letters and Diaries*, 11:278.
[51] Ibid.

Even though Newman and Manzoni never personally met each other, they had many similarities in their lives and in their spiritual beliefs. In his work *Newman: Il Coraggio della Verità*, Father Giovanni Velocci described these affinities: "Both converts, both Christians of profound faith and faithful attachment to the Church, both men of high culture, involved in the search for truth." [52] In fact, Newman seemed inspired by how much he and Manzoni had in common, and he searched for ways to connect himself with Manzoni.

Newman was aware of the fact that both he and Manzoni had experienced transformational conversions. While Newman's first conversion was in the autumn of 1816 at the age of fifteen, Manzoni "first felt the divine intervention listening to sacred music in the church of Saint Roch, into which he had wandered one day in April 1810 (during a public celebration of Napoleon's marriage to Marie Louise), dizzy and nervous, having lost his wife in the crowd, and desperately asking God to give him proof of His existence." [53] Furthermore, in 1833 Newman and Manzoni both had other life-altering conversion experiences resulting from personal trials. "For Newman the cross to be borne was his illness in Sicily when Newman thought he was so sick that he was going to die. While, in Manzoni's case, his tribulation lay in having to cope with the death of his beloved wife, Enrichetta Blondel." [54]

In addition, Newman seemed to be inspired by Manzoni's strong belief in the power of both the Catholic Faith and of God's Providence to lead human beings through the vicissitudes of life. This spiritual certitude was very comforting to the troubled John Henry Newman as he read *I Promessi Sposi*. He wrote to his sister Jemima that in the novel he had discovered "a depth of religious feeling. . . . It quite transported me." [55]

[52] Giovanni Velocci, C.SS.R., *Newman: Il Coraggio della Verità* (Vatican City: Libreria Editrice Vaticana, 2000), 216.

[53] Barricelli, *Alessandro Manzoni*, 19.

[54] Nicholas L. Gregoris, *"The Daughter of Eve Unfallen": Mary in the Theology and Spirituality of John Henry Newman* (Mount Pocono, Pa.: Newman House Press, 2003), 29.

[55] Newman, "To Jemima," *Letters and Diaries*, 6:150.

Examples such as the following must have been moving and convincing statements to Newman at a time when they were most needed:

> One of the strangest faculties of the Christian religion, and one of the hardest to understand, is her power of giving direction and consolation to everyone who has recourse to her, in no matter what circumstances, at no matter what time. If there is a remedy for what is past, she prescribes it, and gives us the vision and the strength to carry it out, whatever the cost. If there is no remedy, she shows us how to make a literal reality of the proverbial expression "to make a virtue of necessity." She teaches us to continue wisely in the course we entered upon out of frivolity. She chastens our heart to accept gladly that which is imposed on us by tyranny, she gives a reckless but irrevocable choice all the sanctity, all the wisdom, all the—let us say it—all the joyful happiness of a true vocation. She is like a great road, which a man may find after wandering in the most tangled labyrinth, amid the most dangerous precipices, and once he had taken one stride along it, he can walk on safely and gladly, and be sure of a happy end to his journey.[56]

One can speculate that Newman might have read these writings of Manzoni and longed to take the "great road" toward Catholicism, where he could be assured of a "happy end to his journey."

Further, there is definite evidence in Newman's works to indicate that he did share Manzoni's trust in God's Providence. Newman even expressed himself in a similar manner although his Providence flowed directly from God rather than through the Church:

> How gracious is the revelation of God's particular providence to those who seek Him! How gracious to those who have discovered that this world is but vanity, and who are solitary and isolated in themselves, whatever shadows of power and happiness surround them! The multitude, indeed, go on without these thoughts, either from insensibility, as not understanding their own wants, or changing from one idol to another, as each successively fails. But men of keener

[56] Manzoni, *The Betrothed*, trans. Bruce Penman, 203–204.

hearts would be overpowered by despondency, and would even loathe existence, did they suppose themselves under the mere operation of fixed laws, powerless to excite the pity or the attention of Him who has appointed them.[57]

"Newman and Manzoni had a secure faith in Providence; they made it one of the foundations of their thought, and they saw it in action even in the little facts of history." [58]

Therefore, John Henry Newman certainly admired Alessandro Manzoni and learned from him about Catholic concepts and traditions. But, perhaps, most of all, Manzoni helped to turn Newman's heart towards the Catholic Faith. The biographer Sheridan Gilley has said that Newman's writing about the Capuchin, Fra Cristoforo during the difficult years of the Via Media was significant—"It was almost as if his anti-Roman polemic was an emotional defense against a reluctant sympathy." [59]

In fact, Newman was never to forget Manzoni, and he mentioned the Italian often to his friends. Many years later, when Newman was in the throes of writing *The Apologia*, one of his fellow priests and Oratorians, Father Ryder, described the difficulty of the project by quoting Manzoni's poem *In Morte di Napoleone* (On the Occasion of the Death of Napoleon):

The effort of writing the weekly parts was overpowering. On such occasions he wrote through the night, and he has been found with his head in his hands crying like a child over the, to him, well-nigh impossibly painful task of public confession:

> *'Tal su quell' alma il cumulo*
> *Delle memorie scese.*
> *Oh! quante volte ai posteri*
> *Narrar se stesso imprese,*
> *E sulle eterne pagine*
> *Cadde la stanca man!* [60]

[57] John Henry Newman, *Parochial and Plain Sermons*, vol. 3 (New York: Longmans, Green & Co., 1907), 123.

[58] Velocci, *Newman: Il Coraggio*, 31.

[59] Sheridan Gilley, *Newman and His Age* (London: Darton, Longman and Todd, 1990), 186.

[60] Wilfred Ward, *Life of . . . Newman*, 2:23.

In fact, these words of Manzoni when translated into the English certainly were appropriate to describe the anguish that Newman felt as he tried to explain his life:

> *Heavy on that soul the weight*
> *Of memories descending*
> *How often for posterity*
> *He began to write his story*
> *And on the eternal pages*
> *His weary hand would fall.* [61]

Newman was never to lose his respect for Manzoni and his works and, most specifically, for the character of Fra Cristoforo. When Newman made his famous speech at the opening of St. Bernard's Seminary in 1873, he spoke of the Catholic priest as the vehicle for "handing down of the truth from generation to generation. . . . Each circle of Christians has its own priest, who is the representative of the divine idea to that circle in its theological and ethical aspects. He teaches his people, he catechizes their children, bringing them one and all into that form of doctrine, which is his own." [62]

Surely, this portrait was reminiscent of Manzoni's Fra Cristoforo who was a true representative of the divine idea as he instructed the young couple on the responsibilities of a Christian marriage:

> You [Lucia] must pray again for the divine grace that you prayed for in the beginning, to help you to be a holy wife. You must have faith that he will grant you that grace in even fuller measure, after all that you have suffered. And you, Renzo, he went on, turning towards the young man, remember this: if the Church now gives you back this companion in life, she does not do so to provide you with a temporal and earthly happiness, which, even if perfect in its kind and without any admixture of bitterness, must still finish in a

---

[61] Translated in Bernard Wall, *Alessandro Manzoni* (New Haven: Yale University Press, 1954), 19.

[62] John Henry Newman, "The Infidelity of the Future," in *Faith and Prejudice and Other Unpublished Sermons of Cardinal Newman* (New York: Sheed & Ward, 1956), 114–115.

great sorrow when the time comes for you to leave each other; she does so to set you both on the road to that happiness which had no end. Love each other as fellow-travelers on that road, remembering that you must part some day, and hoping to be reunited later for all time.[63]

Thus, there can be little doubt that Newman was inspired by the works of Alessandro Manzoni, for Newman realized that, through his writings, the Italian author had created a priest who conveyed Catholic Tradition. Manzoni's Cristoforo had the ability to do that which Newman believed in: the "giving over from mouth to mouth as it were—from father to son, what the Apostles spoke! Their teaching was like our catechism and we are to teach now what they taught." [64]

Newman and the Philosopher-Priest Antonio Rosmini

However, Alessandro Manzoni was not the only illustrious Italian with whom Newman wanted to forge a friendship. Ironically, for an Englishman who had had very little affinity towards Italians or association with them for the first forty years of his life, Newman, as a Catholic, seemed to be drawn to famous Italians. During the same visit to Milan in 1846 when he missed meeting Alessandro Manzoni, Newman was also trying to come into contact with another luminary, Antonio Rosmini-Serbati. A philosopher, patriot, and promoter of the Catholic revival in Italy, Rosmini founded the Institute of Charity, or Rosminians, in 1828. The field of work during his lifetime lay almost exclusively in Northern Italy and England, and he and his followers established Ratcliffe College near Loughborough, England.[65] Like Father Dominic and the Passionist Fathers, these Italians, also, felt the need to bring Catholicism to the people of England.

---

[63] Manzoni, *The Betrothed*, trans. Bruce Penman, 682–683.

[64] Manuscripts of J. H. Newman, quoted in Günter Biemer, *Newman on Tradition* (New York: Herder and Herder, 1967), 190.

[65] Charles Stephen Dessain, *The Letters and Diaries of John Henry Newman*, vol. 11 (London: Thomas Nelson and Sons, 1961), 354.

Newman's letters indicate that, quite early in the 1840s, he was aware of Antonio Rosmini and his priests, who were mostly Italian. The connection between Newman and Rosmini was made through Father Luigi Gentili. Born in Rome in 1801, the same year that Newman had been born in England, Gentili early embraced a religious life, and with Cardinal Consalvi as his patron, was ordained in 1830. Soon after, he entered the Rosminian novitiate, and with the Rosminians he went to England in 1835. After working there for several years, Gentili became chaplain to A. L. Phillipps, a man devoted to the cause of the restoration of the Catholic Church in England. Together, Gentili and Phillipps had called on Newman at Oriel on 20 October 1842, and in the same year, Gentili opened the house at Loughborough. "He made many converts in the neighbourhood, and even more when he became an itinerant missionary two years later." Gentili died in 1848.[66]

Father Gentili and the Rosminians were to play an important role in Newman's conversion, and Newman had been introduced to them by his close friend, William Lockhart. After taking his B.A. degree at Exeter College, Lockhart had joined Newman at Littlemore in July of 1842:

> He [Lockhart] was already drawn towards the Catholic Church and realized that Newman hesitated as to his own power to confer the Sacrament of Penance. He promised that he would make no move for three years, but he was so unhappy that in August 1843 he went away to consult Father Gentili, and was received after three days. The defection led Newman to resign his living at St. Mary's and to preach his last Anglican sermon, "the Parting of Friends." Lockhart at once joined the Rosminians and was professed at Ratcliffe College on 8 September 1845. He spent his life as a missioner and writer, known as an exemplary religious and as one full of charity for his former co-religionists. He remained always the disciple of Newman and wrote after his death, *Cardinal Newman: Reminiscences of Fifty Years Since*, by one of his oldest living disciples, London, 1891.[67]

[66] Ibid., 11:341.
[67] Ibid., 11:344–345.

Newman was to visit Lockhart quite often at Ratcliffe College, and in January of 1846, he noted that he and St. John had spent the Feast of the Epiphany with the Rosminians: "Lockhart is quite well again—this is a very handsome building—and the whole ceremonial is handsome. It is small. There is more preciseness and rule than among Father Dominic and his Passionists, with whom St. John and I were last week." [68]

In addition to Newman, other Oxford men were looking towards the Italian orders for sanctuary and guidance, and, later that year, Newman shared this fact with Dalgairns. He told his friend—"This letter is quite in confidence as you will see—but the fact is, Oscott is losing its Divines fast. They slip away. It cannot keep them. This vacation Mr. Swift and Mr. Marshall are going on a trial to Ratcliffe—Montgomery to F. Dominic. . . ." [69] In the same letter, Newman was explaining options that he was considering for the future, and he further discussed the success of the Rosminians. "Then you see, I see nothing except that the notion of a theological school is a great idea—and natural, not only from our hitherto line of reading, but because the Rosminians (whom I cannot quite like) are fast spreading themselves, as givers of retreats and missions, all over England." [70]

Despite Newman's statement that he could not "quite like" the Rosminians, he certainly seemed to express interest in them and in Rosmini himself. When he and St. John arrived in Milan in September of 1846, they were similarly impressed by the Order's work, as in England, and they sought to connect with Antonio Rosmini. Newman noted that "we find ourselves among the friends of Rosmini and are surprised to find how much the Rosminians are doing in these parts. Don't let this be said out of Maryvale. Perhaps we shall learn some more, and you shall know all of it. We have a letter to Rosmini, but he is some way off." [71]

[68] Newman, "To R. W. Church," *Letters and Diaries*, 11:85.
[69] Newman, "To J. D. Dalgairns," *Letters and Diaries*, 11:195.
[70] Ibid., 11:196.
[71] Newman, "To W. G. Penny," *Letters and Diaries*, 11:249.

There can be no doubt that, on the surface, Newman expressed a certain distrust of Rosmini, but, likewise, he also had a fascination for the man and his accomplishments. Unfortunately, Newman was never to meet Rosmini in person. "Rosmini passed through Milan, sending me a civil message, with an explanation that he did not call since he could not speak Latin nor I Italian. This is not enough to explain his not calling. Ghianda [Manzoni's chaplain] has a great admiration for him, and Manzoni has also. I wish we had more to tell of him—but I cannot get at the bottom of his philosophy. I wish to believe it is all right, yet one has one's suspicion." [72]

Newman continued to comment in his letters about the complexity of Rosmini's theology, and he certainly wanted "to believe it is all right." Probably, he truly felt within himself an affinity for Rosmini, and he wanted validation for those feelings. And, as Newman spent more time in Italy, he began to realize that there was much to admire in Rosmini's work. Towards the end of that year, he again wrote to Dalgairns. "We heard in Milan that Rosmini's one *idea* was to make a positive substantive philosophy, for at present there was none. Several things of the same kind, that he said, struck me as good. What we hear here, though we have but just begun to hear, confirms this." [73] Newman received further confirmation from a Superior whom he met in Rome that his instincts towards Rosmini were accurate. Newman gave a report about this meeting to Dalgairns. "We have been hearing Mass this morning in the very room of St. Francis (Assisi) in the Trastevere. The Superior is a learned man, one of the Congregation of the Index, and we had some interesting talk with him. . . . [According to the Superior] Rosmini was an able, holy man—a great friend of his own, but had made theology somewhat too philosophical—i.e., wished to prove everything. (It seems one of R's works, *De Conscientia, is* under consideration of the Congregation of the Index.)" [74]

[72] Newman, "To J. D. Dalgairns," *Letters and Diaries*, 11:262–263.
[73] Ibid., 11:279.
[74] Newman, "To J. D. Dalgairns," *Letters and Diaries*, 12:7.

In fact, Newman seemed somewhat defensive of Rosmini when he, himself, was worried that his own University Sermons would, likewise, be subject to inspection and possible condemnation. He again voiced his concern to Dalgairns: "I am terribly frightened lest the book, like Rosmini's and others, should be brought before the Index. . . . I am not maintaining what I say is all true, but I wish to *assist in investigating* and bringing to light *great principles* necessary for the day—and the only way to bring them out is *freely* to investigate, with the inward habitual intention (which I trust I have) always to be submitting what I say to the judgment of the Church." [75]

Through these travails, John Henry Newman began to understand and to appreciate that Antonio Rosmini was, like himself, a man who wanted to bring "to light great principles" that were important in the transmission of Catholic Tradition. As Newman added about his own works—"And now after reading these sermons, I must say I think they are, as a whole, the best things I have written, and I cannot believe that they are not Catholic, and will not be useful." [76]

Although Newman never met Rosmini in person, he recognized that Rosmini was a prominent Catholic theologian. In addition, having spent time with several Rosminians, Newman probably also knew something about their founder's background. Antonio Rosmini was only four years older than Newman, and he was born in Rovereto in northern Italy in 1797. He died at Stresa, on the shores of Lake Maggiore, in 1855. In Rome, today, there is a Collegio Rosmini, and there are Rosmini houses around the world. These institutes are constantly promoting the Cause for the Beatification of Rosmini. Their literature effectively summarizes the life of Antonio Rosmini:

> He heard God's call at a young age and became a priest in 1821. He devoted his considerable academic gifts to the service of God and the Church. Pope Pius VIII told him in 1829 that God was calling him to write books. Pope Gregory

[75] Ibid., 12:29.
[76] Ibid., 12:32.

XVI, who held him in high regard, said the same thing. Rosmini remained faithful to this particular vocation despite difficulties and misunderstandings his works sometimes provoked. Blessed Pius IX was another patron of Rosmini. With his wide-ranging intellect, Rosmini tackled the leading questions in theology and philosophy of his day. Alessandro Manzoni, the most famous Italian writer of the time and Rosmini's close friend, said of him: "He is one of the six or seven brightest minds that honour humanity." He wrote well over a hundred books, dealing not just with theology and philosophy, but also education, law, politics, the defense of the Faith and the spiritual life. He was driven to this prodigious output by his love of truth and his love of his fellow human beings.

Many people, especially Saint Maddalena di Canossa, urged him to found a religious order. Convinced that this was God's will, he founded the Institute of Charity on Mount Calvary, Domodossola. The order was approved by Pope Gregory XVI in 1839 and is usually known as the Rosminians. As well as Priests and Brothers, Rosmini nurtured within the Institute a branch of Sisters, and lay men and women known as the Ascribed who share the life of Rosminian spirituality.[77]

From this description, one can envision Antonio Rosmini as the Italian John Henry Newman. For, Newman was also a philosopher, a writer, and a priest. Also, like Newman, Rosmini had had an education which included a study of both the Church Fathers and the people of the Enlightenment. A twentieth-century leader of the Rosminians, Father General Giuseppe Bozzetti, has said that there is a rising influence of Rosmini's philosophy among Italian university professors and students:

> They have found in Rosmini a man who, though bound to the past, understood the vitality and the insistence of the modern mind, which he had mastered and used while remaining a powerful advocate of the perennial values of traditional thought. Thus Rosmini not only studied Descartes,

---

[77] Father James Flynn (Father General), *Antonio Rosmini: Man of God*, vol. 2 (Rome: Collegio Rosmini, n.d.), 4.

Spinoza, Leibnitz, Locke, Berkeley, Reid, Hume, Kant, Fichte, Schelling, and Hegel, but he understood them, saw the reason for their influence, entered into a consideration of the problems that they raised and was thus able to "speak their language," and enter into a real discussion. What was more important, he could show appreciation for all that was alive and true in their contributions to the unceasing flow of philosophic thought, even as he could judge their deficiencies and limitations. At the same time he lost nothing of the intellectual treasures of the Middle Ages, which the modern mentality either refuses to look at or condemns as out of date.

Such was the grandiose enterprise of Rosmini; he endeavoured to weld the fracture between Christian Tradition and the contemporary mind. Only time can tell how far he has succeeded. Manzoni said that Rosmini was born fifty years too soon: we might safely treble the figure. His attempt was indeed noble, but it can be easily understood how Rosmini met opposition from both the sides that he was seeking to reconcile. It is the common fate of great men to find reprobation and condemnation from those whom they seek to benefit, even though appreciation follows in the course of time.[78]

Therefore, Antonio Rosmini was an Italian intellectual who respected and understood the foremost philosophical minds of his era, and yet his modern outlook never diminished his love of the Catholic Faith and its Tradition. As Father Bozzetti summarized Rosmini's religious inspiration—"Like Newman, he was a man for whom all that was thought or felt could not be seen or understood except in the light and love of the Christ-God. One of the greatest Christians of his time, what was peculiarly his was a capacity for including everything in his religious vision without in any way changing a single essential characteristic of what he saw." [79]

Italians have long been fascinated with the similarities between Newman and Rosmini. As Antonio Patrone said in his article about the missed meeting between the two: "For one

---

[78] Giuseppe Bozzetti, introduction to Claude Leetham, *Rosmini: Priest, Philosopher and Patriot* (London: Longmans, Green and Co., 1957), xvi–xvii.

[79] Ibid., xxii.

who has studied in some fashion the thought and life of Rosmini and that of Newman, it is easy to establish that Rosmini is to Italy what Newman is to England. And for those who are knowledgeable, this relationship can seem obvious." [80] Patrone continued by discussing the relationship between the two men. Rosmini certainly knew Newman through the happenings of the Oxford Movement. The Rosminian Fathers had already arrived in England by 1835, and they followed the Movement carefully, sensing that it could be an excellent area of conversions to the Catholic Church. Therefore, Fathers Luigi Gentili and Giovanni Pagani gave Rosmini ample reports of the activity of the Movement and of their personal involvements in connection with its members. [81]

Patrone continued his essay by citing several instances in which Rosmini mentioned Newman in letters to Pusey, Gentili, and Pagani. Rosmini's knowledge of Newman increased as the Movement got more and more publicity. Early in 1846, Rosmini wrote to Pagani that he was greatly consoled by the news of the recent converts from Oxford to Catholicism and that he knew they would bring glory to God and blessings to England. In another letter of the same year, he wrote in a very complimentary manner about the contents of the *Essay on the Development of Christian Doctrine*: "It seems to me that the work [*Essay on the Development of Christian Doctrine*] is original and that it manifests a very noble undertaking. He [Newman] began the work before becoming Catholic, and he ended it after having embraced Catholicism." [82]

Therefore, there is certainly evidence that Antonio Rosmini knew John Henry Newman and had read several of his works. Yet, probably, Newman was much more familiar with Rosmini:

> Newman instead knows Rosmini in an almost direct way and much more profoundly. In fact, he had heard Rosmini speak to Rosminians before his conversion during colloquia

---

[80] Antonio Patrone, "Rosmini-Newman: un incontro mancato tra due personalità filosofiche," *Oratorium* (1976), 52–53.

[81] Ibid., 53.

[82] Antonio Rosmini; quoted in Patrone, "Rosmini-Newman," 55.

which Rosmini had had with them. At Littlemore, a little village not far from Birmingham, where Newman retired after he gave up his post at the parish of St. Mary's in Oxford, the Rosminians had to feel almost at home. . . . And from the discussions with Father Gentili, Newman would have known something of the philosophy of Rosmini. . . . However, the knowledge of Rosmini on the part of Newman came through his works. At Littlemore, in that quasi-religious community that Newman had gathered about him, Newman adopted the use of Rosmini's works, *The Manual of the Retreatant* and *The Maxims of Christian Perfection*. These are works that served Newman's purposes at that particular moment, but by means of such works Newman would have been able to know the sanctity of Rosmini and would have remained fascinated by him.[83]

Newman did remain fascinated with Rosmini, although he acknowledged that he did not understand completely the Italian's philosophy. Even though the meeting between Newman and Rosmini never took place, and Rosmini was to die only nine years later, Newman mentioned, for the remainder of his life, the affinity he had towards Rosmini.

Even after he returned to England as a Catholic priest, Newman would continue to encounter the works of Rosmini and to refer to them. In 1849 Newman was asked by Cardinal Wiseman "as a great favour," to "look over Rosmini's new book *Cinque Piaghe* [The Five Wounds of the Church] . . . and mark passages." [84] Later that year, Newman would write, "I fear some row is coming on about Rosmini's *Five Wounds of the Church*. Don't repeat it. I respect his people so much, that I am very sorry for it." [85]

Five years later when at a meeting of the Holy Office, presided over by Blessed Pius IX, it was decided that there was nothing in Rosmini's works deserving of censure, Newman seemed very pleased and quoted a communication from Rosmini giving the welcome information: "I received authentic

[83] Patrone, "Rosmini-Newman," 56–57.
[84] *Letters and Diaries*, 13:188.
[85] Newman, "To Miss M. R. Giberne," *Letters and Diaries*, 13:239.

information that the result of the examination of my works in Rome was determined to be *nihil inventum est censura dignum* [without anything worthy of censorship]. If afterwards my works are to be published, when and how, that is not yet known." [86]

Unfortunately, Antonio Rosmini-Serbati died on July 1 of that same year, and his hopes of further publications would not come true. On July 10, Newman wrote a letter of condolence to Father Pagani in which he said he feared that Rosmini's sufferings had shortened his life. "I'm writing a few lines to Your Reverence to express my sorrow with you and with your priests on the occasion of the loss of your renowned and holy Founder. . . . A man like him while on earth was the property of the whole Church." [87]

Therefore, because Newman saw Rosmini as being the property of the world-wide Church, and the Rosminian Order did much of its early work in England, the Italians themselves take great pride in linking Rosmini and Newman. On the hundredth anniversary of Newman's death, Francesco Cossiga, the then-President of the Italian Republic, wrote an essay detailing the connection:

> It is certain that Newman respected and admired Rosmini; he too had lived under a cloud. In his private diary, Newman has strong words of condemnation for the way in which Rosmini had been treated by the ecclesiastical authorities.
>
> . . . Newman and Rosmini were two great masters who fought in defense of truth and Christianity. . . . Both of them were Christian thinkers of depth and power. Faith for them, in other words, was not a substitute for reason, but itself a source of knowledge which enjoyed a delicate and complex alliance with reason. Anything less they saw as a threat to the integrity of Christian believing. Thus Rosmini, according to the title of one of his posthumously published works, opposed "rationalism, that attempts to insinuate itself into the theological schools," and Newman, speaking in Rome in 1879, could point to his lifelong stand against liberalism, by

---

[86] Newman, "Miss Giberne," *Letters and Diaries*, 16:213.
[87] Ibid., 16:504–505.

which he meant "the doctrine that there is no positive truth in religion, but that one creed is as good as another."

... Newman and Rosmini emerge today as two exalted spirits, two prophets and pioneers in the Church, who suffered for their love of truth.[88]

Therefore, these two "prophets and pioneers in the Church" certainly shared some common ideas concerning doctrinal development, the importance of Providence, and faith and reason. The first of Rosmini's theological books to be translated into English, *Theological Language,* includes a strong testimony to the fact that Newman and Rosmini had similar ideas about the development of doctrine: [89]

There is nothing more abhorrent to heretics than the natural, enlightened development brought about by the Church in the deposit of faith during the course of centuries. This development has ensured the continued identity of the deposit in the midst of new and ever more splendid expressions; it has gone hand in hand with the development of worship which, as part of Catholicism, has been able with its majestic splendour to attract, move and conquer heretics themselves, despite their prejudices. Amongst these heretics, some recognized the error in which they had been raised. Men of good will and able minds, although brought up on the false principle that every innovation in the Church is a deviation from primitive evangelical teaching, were able to reflect and see that the Church of Christ, which is not a corpse but a society living throughout the ages, possesses its own natural development as a consequence of its vital state. It was this thread of life which drew them along the way leading to entry into the Catholic Church. Two especially come to mind: Karl Ludwig von Haller who, despite his inborn prejudices, clearly recognized that the Christian religion is like a seed containing in itself the future tree (like the mustard seed that would develop throughout the ages), and embraced the truth without further difficulty, as he himself says in various places in his writings; and John

---

[88] Francesco Cossiga, "Newman the Man," in *Newman: A Man for Our Time,* ed. David Brown (Harrisburg, Pa.: Morehouse Publishing, 1990), 22–23.

[89] Rosmini began this work in 1854 but did not complete it before his death. The manuscript lay unpublished until 1880, and even then it was not published in its entirety. Only in 1975 did it appear in its full form in Italian.

Henry Newman who, on the basis of the natural development of Christian doctrine and practice, wrote the book that
signaled his future conversion.[90]

Clearly, Rosmini admired the work that Newman had done
on development, and, likewise, the Italian's strong belief in the
Catholic Church as the transmitter of faith would be very useful
for Newman. In addition, Newman seemed to be drawn to the
zeal of these Italians who were not afraid to place their destinies
in the hand of God. For "like Rosmini, he had a very positive
idea of 'divine Providence.'"[91] In fact, from the day of his first
conversion (12 April 1822), Newman felt that his life was ordered by God to its true end and purpose. He never wavered
from this absolute certainty in God's plan: "Henceforth his way
was clear before him; and he was constant all through his life, as
his intimate friends know, in his thankful remembrance year
after year of this great mercy of Divine Providence."[92] Thereafter, Newman would often make reference in his works and
his letters to the fact that he believed his life was preordained
according to the will of God.

Likewise, Rosmini had an inherent belief in God's Providence, and he would mention this certainty to his followers,
especially those who had the difficult missions abroad. In a
letter to Don Antonio Rey at Prior Park in England on 7 August
1836, he said:

> My dear companion in God's service,
> Your welcome letter of 18 June made me consider seriously
> what can be the cause of the anxieties you suffer and the
> persistency with which they recur. I should so like to find
> some remedy for them, so that you may enjoy peace of mind
> and sanctify yourself in the vocation which you have ac-
> cepted. So take careful heed and see whether the advice I
> am going to give you comes from God, as I firmly believe it
> does.

[90] Antonio Rosmini, *Theological Language*, trans. Denis Cleary (Durham, England: Rosmini House, 2004), 42.

[91] Lord St. John of Fawsley, "Newman: A Portrait," in *Newman: A Man for Our Time*, 25.

[92] *Autobiographical Writings*, 63.

> The reasons for your troubles are: (1) you have not yet fully grasped that *outside yourself there is for you neither good nor evil, but all your true good lies in your own sanctification*; (2) you have not yet fully grasped that *external things (whether good or bad) which do not depend on your own will can be and indeed are, in the hands of Divine Providence, so many means of increasing your holiness.*[93]

Antonio Rosmini was writing to his people in England to have faith in God's Divine Providence, and the Rosminians who were the recipients of their founder's advice and consolation were the same people with whom Newman had had contact before and after his conversion.

In addition, Newman's ideas on faith and reason were certainly consistent with those expressed by Rosmini in 1850:

> What seems to merit greatest attention, however, is the sign given by Augustine for recognizing those who have the capacity for undertaking this kind of study and, by philosophizing about God, adding more light, through good use of the speculative mind, to what is taught by authority. The standard is this: their capacity for arriving at an understanding of that which forms pure mind, pure intelligence. Only knowledge of the nature of the mind, an element of our soul, can be applied to the Creator in such a way as to make possible some kind of reasoning about the Being Who is above all creation. Those who cannot grasp this doctrine of the mind and intelligence should be content with faith; their souls falter in their own sight, and fail to recognize what is best in themselves, that is, their intellectual element.[94]

In 1870, Newman was to state, likewise, that the investigation of a religious concept did not indicate a lack of faith. "Therefore, to set about concluding a proposition is not *ipso facto* to doubt its truth; we may aim at inferring a proposition, while all the time we assent to it. We have to do this as a common occurrence, when we take on ourselves to convince another on any point in which he differs from us. We do not deny our own

[93] Antonio Rosmini, *The Ascetical Letters*, vol. 2 (Loughborough, England: John Morris, Our Lady's Convent, 1995), 244.

[94] Rosmini, *Theological Language*, 18–19.

faith, because we become controversialists." [95] Further, Newman also agreed with Rosmini that it was the duty of thinking people to apply reason to their beliefs. Newman expressed this responsibility: "Next, I consider that, in the case of educated minds, investigations into the argumentative proof of the things to which they have given their assent, is an obligation, or rather a necessity. Such a trial of their intellects is a law of their nature, like the growth of childhood into manhood, and analogous to the moral ordeal which is the instrument of their spiritual life." [96]

Therefore, Newman certainly realized that, on a theological level, he had agreed with and learned from Rosmini, and he was anxious that they should have a further interchange in Italy. Although this meeting was not to be, Newman was always to acknowledge the debt that he owed to Rosmini, and Newman would speak of Rosmini in a very positive manner. As he summed up his feelings to Dalgairns—"We heard in Milan that Rosmini's one idea was to make a positive substantive philosophy, for at present there was none. Several things of the same kind, that he said, struck me as good." [97] In addition, the tribute that Newman wrote on the occasion of Rosmini's death so impressed the Italians that Newman was mentioned in the earliest biography of Rosmini. In his 1880 work, *Della Vita di Antonio Rosmini-Serbati* (From the Life of Antonio Rosmini-Serbati), Francesco Paoli described Newman as "Doctor Henry Newman, President of the University of Dublin, now a Most Eminent Cardinal." [98]

The distinguished Doctor Newman was not the only one to be saddened by the death of Rosmini. Upon hearing of the passing of his long-time friend, Alessandro Manzoni "wrote to his wife on July 1: 'My dear, this morning I heard in the Gospel

[95] John Henry Newman, *An Essay in Aid of a Grammar of Assent* (Westminster, Md.: Christian Classics, 1973), 190.

[96] Ibid., 192.

[97] Newman, "To J. D. Dalgairns," *Letters and Diaries*, 11:279.

[98] Francesco Paoli, *Della Vita di Antonio Rosmini-Serbati* (Torino: Dall'Academia di Roverto, 1880), 555.

of the Mass the words *Consummatum est,* that so fitted my awful state of mind, and they urged and encouraged me to go to the source of all consolation. . . . As for the brethren: 'The Lord will help you, for you have walked with His saint, and you have returned blessed in Heaven by His saint, and what a welcome he will have had in Heaven. . . . But we . . . what a desert.'" [99] The lives of John Henry Newman and Alessandro Manzoni were indeed diminished by the passing of Antonio Rosmini.

And, ironically, even after the death of John Henry New- man, he and Rosmini would be forever linked together. As they both had been scrutinized and criticized in life, so would they both be lauded many years after their passing from this life. In Pope John Paul II's Encyclical Letter of 15 September 1998, *Fides et Ratio,* we read: "We see the same fruitful relationship between philosophy and the Word of God in the courageous research pursued by more recent thinkers, among whom I gladly mention, in a Western context, such as John Henry Newman, Antonio Rosmini. . . ." [100] Further affirmation for Ros- mini came in 2001, when the then-Cardinal Joseph Ratzinger said that "it has to be recognized that widespread, serious and rigorous scientific literature on the thought of Anthony Rosmini has shown that the interpretations contrary to Catholic doc- trine and faith do not really correspond to the authentic posi- tion of Rosmini." [101] Once again, Newman was clearly ahead of his time as he attempted to learn about Catholic doctrine from Rosmini.

[99] Claude Leetham, *Rosmini: Priest, Philosopher and Patriot* (London: Longmans, Green and Co., 1957), 480.

[100] Pope John Paul II, *Fides et Ratio: To the Bishops of the Catholic Church on the Relation- ship between Faith and Reason* (15 September 1998), no. 74.

[101] Cardinal Joseph Ratzinger, "Note on the Force of the Doctrinal Decrees con- cerning the Thought and Work of Father Antonio Rosmini Serbati" (1 July 2001), no. 2.

VI

THE LIFELONG GUIDANCE OF PERRONE AND NERI

Newman and the Theologian Giovanni Perrone

Alessandro Manzoni and Antonio Rosmini were definitely positive influences upon Newman, but, unfortunately, he never got to meet them during his first trip to Italy as a Catholic. However, there were two other Italians whom he did encounter (one personally and the other through his followers) during those same years, and these men would be especially significant. The first was Giovanni Perrone, a contemporary theologian who became his friend and advisor, and the other was Saint Philip Neri, the sixteenth-century Christian humanist, who would be his inspiration for becoming an Oratorian.

While Saint Philip was the ideal, Perrone would be the real-life figure to whom Newman would turn when he arrived in Rome. For one reason or another, Manzoni and Rosmini had both avoided personal contact with the visiting Englishman. In fact, Newman did not wholly believe Rosmini's excuse for not meeting him, and there is speculation that Rosmini in some manner had known that there was not full acceptance in Rome of the themes of Newman in his Essay on the Development of Christian Doctrine. "In fact, the first perplexities that Newman had in Rome came about immediately, and, in February of 1847, he submitted the book and the contents of the University Sermons, in the form of a thesis, to Father Perrone, the Jesuit professor of dogmatic theology at the Roman College." [1]

---

[1] Antonio Patrone, "Rosmini-Newman: un incontro mancato tra due personalità filosofiche," *Oratorium* (1976), 63.

The man who would first offer help to John Newman during those early days in Italy and for the remainder of their lives was one of the most famous theologians of that era. Father Giovanni Perrone was a Jesuit whose longevity (1794–1876) almost mirrored that of Newman.

> He [Perrone] was Professor of Dogmatic Theology at the Roman College 1824–30, 1834–48. In the latter year, he was driven into exile for three years, spent at St. Beuno's in Wales, by the Roman Revolution, returning to be Rector of the Roman College, and remaining in Rome for the rest of his life. Perrone did not at first understand Newman, but in 1847 they came closer together, and Newman drew up for him theses on Development. . . . He defended Newman in Rome, notably in 1867. His best known work *Praelectiones Theologicae* went into 34 editions, and the later ones had a note that Newman had now embraced the Catholic religion "cujus lumen et columen praeclarissimum evasit, imo, et quodammodo martyr." [2]

In fact, Newman was to learn about Perrone even before he went to Italy. In July of 1846, Newman had a long talk with another Englishman who had also studied in Rome. Thomas Tierney Fergusson became a Catholic in 1838, went to Rome to study, and was ordained in March of 1844. "In June 1844, he called at Littlemore with Father Dominic." [3]

Once again, Newman's Italian connection helped to prepare him for his life as a Catholic. Through Dominic Barberi, he met Fergusson who gave him information about being a student at the College of Propaganda. Fergusson's advice was both practical and educational. Newman discussed what he had learned in a letter to Ambrose St. John:

> . . . Next, you may not have *clothes* of your own—the Rector takes away coat, trousers, shirts, stockings, etc. etc. and gives you some of the Propaganda's. "Then it is no use," I said, "taking a portmanteau." No, said Dr. F., it is no use. They

[2] Charles Stephen Dessain, "Index of Persons and Places," in *Letters and Diaries*, 11:351–352.
[3] Ibid., 11:340.

give you two cassocks, an *old* one and a new one. It is a great object to use up the old clothes. Mr. Eyre (who was present) even said, though I suppose it was fun, that they gave you old shoes. Why, one might catch the plague, for depend on it, there are Egyptians and Turks there.

Yes, they are from all nations—except English. Dr. F. said there was not a single Englishman all the time he was there.

To complete it, he said that I shall be kept there three years, and that I should have to read Perrone.[4]

As soon as Newman arrived in Rome, he realized that an acquaintance with Father Perrone would, indeed, be quite useful to him. In one of his first letters from the College of Propaganda, he seemed excited to tell Dalgairns: "What do you think Father Perrone in his new edition says of me? 'Newman Romanum Pontificem vocat diabolum.' By the bye it is an encouraging fact, connected with the theory of development, that the said Perrone is writing a book to show that the Immaculate Conception may be made an article of faith."[5]

Even though there is conjecture that Perrone did not fully understand Newman's work on development, Newman was still honored to have been recognized by the famous Italian theologian. In a further letter to Dalgairns a few weeks later, Newman mentioned that his instructor at Propaganda had discussed Perrone and his ideas about Catholic Tradition:

> Perrone (in what we are reading in lecture) maintains that the canon fixed at Trent depends *solely* on the Tradition of the Roman Church—he simply gives up Catholic Tradition. I asked the lecturer if it was not so—he did not like to admit it, and said the Tradition *principalium ecclesiarum* was necessary but not of the *particular* churches (he is most surprisingly fluent in Latin). I asked whether in the case of the canon there was *any* tradition but that of Rome but I could not get him to say yes or no (don't tell all this to a soul) I went on to ask whether the Church might not define that inspiration was only *quoad res et sententias*—he said it might—then I asked whether, since (as he had said in lectures) Fathers and

[4] Newman, "To Ambrose St. John," *Letters and Diaries*, 11:200–201.
[5] Newman, "To J. D. Dalgairns," *Letters and Diaries*, 11:275.

divines up to Trent held verbal inspiration, the Church would not in that case define a point *without* Tradition. I could not get him to throw any light upon the matter. All this was in private—next day in lecture he took care to observe that traditions *might have* existed which were not lost—(and he almost said it was *de fide* to hold or at least that a Catholic would hold, that the Fathers always *did* go by Tradition. I would not be sure he said this however—this he said, that at least they were inerrable in Council, so *it was no matter.*) As if the hypothesis of *lost* traditions could account for the Fathers writing the *contrary*! All this shows how little they have of a view.[6]

Thus, Newman was anxious to learn from the Italians whether they felt that Tradition could have existed outside of the Catholic Church, and, as he stated, he wanted to address the issue with Giovanni Perrone. Newman knew that his ordination was close at hand, and he needed to glean as much information as he could from the theologians who were instructing him. "They have the power in Propaganda of conferring orders close together—and I suppose they might ordain us Subdeacon, Deacon, and Priest in three successive weeks. Meanwhile considering there is so much to read and think about, we are glad to remain as we are. The great theologians here are the Jesuits at the Collegio Romano and a Dominican."[7] Of course, one of the great Jesuit theologians of whom he spoke was Perrone. As Bouyer described his importance to Newman:

> The Jesuit Perrone—he and his like—who had retained, or renewed, contact with a sorely decaying scholastic tradition, would have furnished the only, or almost the only, example of a Catholic thinker who was not a mere amateur. Now, apart from Tradition, there is no Catholic theology, for Catholic theology is but the voice of Tradition taking stock of itself in the minds of those whom it has fed and watered. But how was Tradition to be preserved in a world where all the schools that had ensured its continuity, at all events since

[6] Ibid., 11:280.
[7] Newman, "To W. G. Penny," *Letters and Diaries*, 11:293.

the Middle Ages, had been expelled or abolished? . . .
Within this general framework, the position of the Catholic
Church in England was peculiar. There it had suffered more
grievously in the past than in any other land. In England,
the most elementary civil rights had only just been restored
to Catholics. Hitherto, they had lived the lives of the down-
trodden, despised, and negligible minority, outside the pale
of society. Small wonder, then, if they still continued to
comport themselves like people perpetually on the defensive, as if, in short, they were handicapped by a chronic
inferiority complex. Debarred from the universities, unable
to give their priests a worthy cultural education, they lived
as it were on the fringe of the world, clinging like wild
creatures to the protection of a sort of ghetto, which, even
when the chance was given them, they showed no disposition to quit.[8]

Therefore, with priesthood looming before him and with his
lack of exposure to Catholic theologians while living in England, Newman had just reason to desire personal contacts
with recognized Italian thinkers like Giovanni Perrone. But
another problem was presenting itself to Newman—the uncertainty of Newman's own position as a theologian. "The leading
dogmatic theologian in Rome, Carlo Passaglia, disapproved of
the *Essay on Development*. There was enough suspicion of the
converts in England without opposition from Rome as well.
Newman had thought of writing a preface to the projected
French translation of the *Essay*, in order to rebut the charge
that he was substituting probability for certainty."[9] However,
he wanted to avoid any further publicity for the book, and he
explained this reluctance to Dalgairns: "I am so timid about
my *Essay* that I have not the heart to hasten its publication
until I have a little more encouragement that I am not, as the
Scotch Dr. Grant here says, in material heresy. . . . I don't like
to begin my career in the Catholic Church with a condemnation or retraction."[10]

[8] Louis Bouyer, *Newman: His Life and Spirituality* (New York: P. J. Kenedy & Sons,
1958), 347–348.
[9] Ian Ker, *John Henry Newman: A Biography* (Oxford University Press, 1988), 329.
[10] Newman, "To J. D. Dalgairns," *Letters and Diaries*, 12:36.

"In the end he decided to send to the other leading theologian in Rome, Giovanni Perrone, a list of formal propositions summarizing his views on faith and reason. He also sent him a paper on his theory of development." [11] Thus, in the spring of 1847, a troubled Newman decided to entrust his work to Perrone, and he enclosed with it the following letter:

> I am sending you herewith those things that you, most excellent sir, with your customary goodwill, have asked from me; however, I believe they are longer than you, with your very great patience, expected. It is difficult even in a long drawn out treatment to accomplish something which, though simple, is nevertheless obscure or new. If by little notes in the margins here or there, if you have free time, you would add your judgment to my labors, it would be a gain to me. I hope I haven't erred, but in matters of this sort, it is easier to hope than to know: this only will I profess, if I may be allowed to repeat it: "I am able to err, but I do not wish to be a heretic." [12]

Newman made a summary in Latin of his views on the development of doctrine, and then Father Perrone added his own comments. This document, which has become known as "The Newman–Perrone Paper on Development," remained unpublished until the 1930s, when the Reverend T. Lynch obtained permission from the Fathers of the Birmingham Oratory and the Rector Magnificus of the Gregorian University, representatives of Cardinal Newman and Father Perrone, respectively. The manuscript consisted of "30 pages of about 12 inches by $8^{1}/_{2}$ in size. The pages were divided into two columns. The one on the left hand was for Newman to write upon, the right-hand one was for Father Perrone's notes. Such was the original plan, but it was not strictly adhered to, for on several occasions Newman's writing overflows into the right-hand column." [13]

[11] Ian Ker, *John Henry Newman*, 330.

[12] Newman, "To Father Perrone, S.J.," *Letters and Diaries*, trans. T. Lynch, 12:40.

[13] Rev. T. Lynch, introduction to "The Newman–Perrone Paper on Development," *Gregorianum* 16 (1935): 402.

The summation of the *Development of Christian Doctrine* that Newman made for Perrone included descriptions of "Chapter I: The Objective Word of God," "Chapter II: The Subjective Word of God," and "Chapter III: The Subjective Word of God in the Catholic Church." Newman explained that the Word of God that belongs to the Catholic Church spread throughout the earth has two aspects: on the one hand it is subjective and on the other it is objective. "It must be said to be objective insofar as it has been or will be transmitted through Christ, the Apostles, the Supreme Pontiff, or Ecumenical Councils into dogmas. The things that are unanimously passed down in every place, not expressly, or by means of any definition, but freely and spontaneously, with a depth of feeling, and a variety of expressions, are subjective to the mind of Catholics."[14] In short, what Newman wanted to submit to Perrone was that "development took place during the unfolding of Christian history and within the Christian consciousness, between two poles: on the one hand, the unique Revelation in Christ Jesus, the *"Verbum Dei Objectivum,"* and, on the other hand, the open, ongoing objectification of this in doctrinal form: the *"Verbum Dei per Ecclesiam Manifestatum."*[15]

Newman then added his twelve theses, including Thesis 11 (in which he discussed the infallibility of the Church when she defines anything in the form of dogma), and Thesis 12 (in which he gave examples of the Church's wisdom in taking her own time to form her definitive judgments). As he told Perrone: "The ancient heretics wanted Aristotle to be joined to theology—with what unfortunate issue! But eventually, after twelve centuries, the Church was divinely led to do just that, to the greatest benefit of Catholics."[16] Thus, the final concept that Newman expressed was that the "Catholic Faith is a dynamic

---

[14] Newman, quoted in Lynch, "The Newman–Perrone Paper on Development," 404–407.

[15] Thomas J. Norris, *Newman and His Theological Method* (Leiden, Netherlands: E. J. Brill, 1977), 162–163.

[16] Newman, quoted in Lynch, "The Newman–Perrone Paper on Development," 443–444.

harmony between growth and permanence, between energetic life and enduring truth. Today it does not exist in a 'static immutability,' but in a 'dynamic continuity,' with the Faith of the Apostles." [17]

Perrone responded to Newman with numerous clarifications, references, and suggestions as to the role of Catholic Tradition in the Development of Christian Doctrine. For Newman's further edification, the Jesuit made a summation of his opinions:

> The things which I have annotated so far may be recalled as follows: 1: that the Church has always been conscious of the whole deposit, divinely committed to her, of all the truths of faith—2: that the deposit has been confided to this same Church as a whole and as one thing—3: that the truths of faith are not susceptible of growth in themselves, but only of being presented with greater explicitness—4: that, for this cause, those truths do not grow materially, as the scholastics speak, and in themselves, but only in the order of our greater knowledge, or a more distinct notion of them through the definition of the Church, and, so to speak, not in regard to themselves, but in regard to us. [18]

Clearly, Newman wanted this type of input and approval from Perrone, who would help Newman to make the transition from the patristic to the Scholastic doctrinal context: "It is true that Newman grew up in the Anglican Church and had been immersed from the start in the Fathers. But in Rome in 1847, he came in contact with Scholastic theologians in the persons of Fathers Passaglia and Perrone, S.J." [19] And Günter Biemer in his work on Tradition has explained Newman's need for Perrone: "There is the well-known fact that Newman did not as a rule propound his theology in technical terms. At the beginning of the theological studies which he undertook in Rome, he took great pains to master scholastic terminology, and Perrone tried to bring Newman's very personal way of expressing

---

[17] Norris, *Newman and His Theological Method*, 163.

[18] Giovanni Perrone, quoted in Lynch, "The Newman–Perrone Paper on Development," 444.

[19] Norris, *Newman and His Theological Method*, 167–168.

himself into line with the language of the schools." [20] Thus, Perrone's participation in and affirmation of Newman's concepts of development gave much legitimacy in Rome to Newman's reputation as a writer and as a theologian.

As his stay lengthened in Rome, Newman continued to seek the advice and even the friendship of Perrone: "I am trying to scrape acquaintance with Perrone. . . . If I have an opening, I shall put before him as clearly as I can my opinions about Faith and Reason." [21] Further, Newman mentioned Perrone several more times in letters to Dalgairns—comments which clearly indicate that Newman was reading Perrone and was trying to learn about the Italian's concepts of faith and reason in addition to Catholic Tradition:

> By the bye, it has struck me sometimes whether perhaps the Tradition of the *Roman* Church may not have been developed *from the first*. St. Irenaeus sends us *to* the see of Rome for the exact faith (as Tertullian does to the Apostolic Churches generally—so that *he* allows a difference and seems to give up strict catholicity.) Perrone, too, as I said in my last, rests the canon on the Roman Tradition, and elsewhere he allows that definitions of faith have been made which were but *implicitly* in the Tradition. . . . Perrone has written a treatise on the connection of Reason and Faith which I like very much. I am glad to see I have no view counter to it, but there is the subtle question, "Whether a person need be conscious of his own certainty (faith)," etc., which I cannot find he answers, and I have asked him about it. [22]

Perrone's work that greatly interested Newman was *Praelectiones Theologicae: Tractatus de Vera Religione adversus Incredulos et Heterodoxos*. This book, which was written in Latin, was designed to answer questions about the veracity of the Catholic Faith. Thus, Chapter One begins with "The Possibility of Divine Revelations" (*sic*), and is followed by explanations to override any difficulties that may be associated with Revelations. [23] New-

[20] Günter Biemer, *Newman on Tradition* (New York: Herder and Herder, 1967), 169.

[21] Newman, "To J. D. Dalgairns," *Letters and Diaries*, 12:55.

[22] Newman, "To J. D. Dalgairns," *Letters and Diaries*, 11:289–290.

[23] Giovanni Perrone, *Praelectiones Theologicae* (Rome: Typis Collegii Urbani, 1840), 3–18.

man's affinity for such knowledge was probably a result of his insecurity about the *University Sermons*. Father Philip Flanagan has said in his book about Newman and faith that the difference in the tone between Newman's Anglican and Catholic writings leads one to suspect that when he wrote the *University Sermons* there was still a defect in his theory on the rationality of faith, and those sermons were his first real attempt at formulating a theory. Further, it was "an attempt made 'with no aid from Anglican and no knowledge of Catholic theologians.' . . . His opinion at that time was probably something like this: Those who accept the evidence for Christianity as conclusive do so because they approach it in the proper spirit. Even if the evidence was less than it is, it would still be sufficient to convince them. On the other hand, those who reject the evidence do so because their dispositions are bad, or because they begin the enquiry with wrong ideas on the possibility of miracles or on some equally vital question." [24]

Flanagan further explained that Newman felt that evidence mattered very little because so much of faith depended on subjective dispositions. Yet, Newman was uneasy about his neglect of some substantive evidence, and when he was in Italy he turned to Perrone to give approval of the *Sermons*, and he used Perrone's writings to substantiate and to enlarge upon his own theories. In fact, in his letter of 8 February 1847, Newman quoted from *Praelectiones Theologicae*: "In Perrone's words, '*nunquam constituere possunt motivum formale actus fidei*.' That reason is necessary for faith." [25]

Newman acknowledged his debt to Perrone and to Rosmini. "At a later date, referring to the question of the proof of religious truth and the reasonableness of certitude, he affirmed: 'When I came to read Catholic theology, I found that it was solved in a way which I felt to be satisfactory.' Newman's Catholic theory on the rationality of faith is to be found in the *University Sermons*. It is there in a distorted form, owing to an

[24] Philip Flanagan, *Faith and the Believer* (London: Sands & Co., 1946), 64–65.
[25] Newman, "To J. D. Dalgairns," *Letters and Diaries*, 12:31.

over-emphasis of one element and the consequent neglect of another." [26]

Thus, it was in Rome that Newman encountered a Catholic theology that would help him to balance faith and reason. The months there were passing very quickly, and he had much to accomplish as a Catholic. On Trinity Sunday, 30 May 1847, he became a priest. As he told Mrs. Bowden, "You will be pleased to hear I was ordained priest about two hours ago; surprised, perhaps, for things have progressed so rapidly that I do not know what I said in my last letter. St. John and I received the subdiaconate last Wednesday, the 26th, St. Philip's day—in Cardinal Fransoni's private chapel—the diaconate yesterday in St. John Lateran—the priesthood today in the Propaganda Church from Cardinal Fransoni. We expect to say our first Mass on Corpus Christi Day." [27]

Beyond his stay in Rome and throughout his priesthood, Newman acknowledged his reliance on Perrone and the importance of Perrone's position as a theologian. From Birmingham in 1849, he wrote to W. G. Ward about the Pope's encyclical *Ubi primum*, which asked the views of the bishops and their flocks as to the question of defining the doctrine of the Immaculate Conception. Newman commented, "I should not mind at a proper time taking part in putting a set of such passages from divines, in spite of what I said about the necessity of eschewing doctrine, *if* I got a man like Perrone to revise what was done— but I would not do it without the highest sanction. You see the Pope has in a way taken up Perrone." [28]

Newman continued his personal friendship and his correspondence with Father Perrone. In fact, Newman was delighted that Perrone was speaking favorably in Rome about the English Oratories. Newman commented in 1850: "Dr. G. [Thomas Grant] speaks of Father Perrone's favorable report of our two Houses." [29] And, again, he was defensive of Perrone

[26] Flanagan, *Faith and the Believer*, 65.
[27] Newman, "To Mrs. J. W. Bowden," *Letters and Diaries*, 12:84–85.
[28] Newman, "To W. G. Ward," *Letters and Diaries*, 13:82.
[29] Newman, "To R. A. Coffin," *Letters and Diaries*, 13:408.

when he responded to F. W. Faber's lectures on English Catholicism:

> As to your papers, they are very clever, and may turn to good account some day, but it seems to me impossible to use them now. They are a simple *direct* attack on the old Catholics. They would be put down too, to bottled up spite—they would lead Anglicans to parallel our position in the Catholic Church with our position in the Protestant—and they would put arms in the hands of our enemies. They are fierce, and nothing but a showing up the old Catholics, and not the least of the Jesuits, and this in the face of Father Perrone's kind report of us at Rome.[30]

As the years went by, Newman and Perrone maintained their mutual respect. In his *Newman–Perrone Paper on Development*, Father Lynch included this appendix:

> The following letter from Perrone to Newman was found in the archives of the Birmingham Oratory: Newman's was found in the archives of the Gregorian University. These two letters form a fitting conclusion to the document upon Development, and show that Perrone, though in private notes to his friend expressing himself with a briefness that sometimes seems not free from asperity, nevertheless fully approved the substantial views of Newman and was ready to undertake his defense when attacked.[31]

This exchange of letters between the two men took place in the spring of 1867. The letter from Perrone was written in Italian and expressed Perrone's continued support for his English friend, even though there had been an outcry that one of Newman's articles, "On Consulting the Faithful," had been denounced for heresy by the Bishop of Newport:[32]

> I suppose that Your Reverence has not forgotten our lovely Italian language, so I am writing you a few lines in this tongue. And first, I thank you for the happy memory that you have continued to keep of me. You cannot believe how

---

[30] Newman, "To F. W. Faber," *Letters and Diaries*, 13:409.

[31] Lynch, "The Newman–Perrone Paper on Development," 445.

[32] Wilfred Ward, *The Life of John Henry Cardinal Newman* (London: Longmans, Green, and Co., 1912), 2:165.

much I have always loved and esteemed Your Reverence. From time to time, I think of you, and I am consoled by the good you have done and continue to do for the benefit of this, your England. . . . I know that Your Reverence has lately had some bitter disappointments, and I have felt them as if they were mine. . . . In some circumstances, I have taken up your defense, and I have been successful. . . . If another occasion should present itself to me, you may be sure that you will always have in me one who will defend your cause. In the course of our life, there are never lacking adversaries who are used by the Lord to prove our fidelity and constancy. But at the end, God will see to it that truth and innocence triumph. . . . I rejoice with the pleasure of having been able with these few lines to converse confidentially with one whom I appreciate so much.[33]

Newman's response to Perrone was written in Latin, indicating that Newman probably did not feel competent to express himself in Italian. Yet, the letter does show the esteem that he felt for Perrone and the strong friendship that these two men had maintained through the years:

I am affected with the fullest joy and the most tender sense of gratitude, most reverend and dearest Father, on account of your letter to me, lately received. For who am I, that after so many years I am still in your memory and heart? And by what means have I deserved to be vindicated and defended so charitably by you? Your defense of me is really of the greatest honor and use to me: nor has it annoyed me to have suffered the petulance of certain rather clever young men, when I am not wholly displeasing to Your Reverence, a man distinguished and subtly versed in the schools of theologians; rather, it is also a consolation to me; for, while I am always well aware that I am not a theologian, I certainly try to the best of my ability to treat the theological matters in my books in a zealous, accurate and cautious way. I rejoice greatly now to be thought of as having written on these matters so as to seem to have pleased, not myself alone, but also you. Please, Most Reverend Father, keep me still in your loving prayers.[34]

[33] Perrone, quoted in Lynch, "The Newman–Perrone Paper on Development," 445–446.
[34] Newman, quoted in ibid., 446–447.

Once again, Newman felt great gratitude that he had had the support of Perrone during a difficult time in his life. Therefore, there can be no doubt that John Henry Newman held Giovanni Perrone in the highest esteem as a friend and as a theologian, and, further, his relationship with Perrone was probably the strongest long-term Italian connection that Newman had maintained. However, Perrone died in 1876, so he was not there in Rome to congratulate his old friend during one of the happiest times in his life—the day that Pope Leo XIII made him a cardinal.

Newman and St. Philip Neri

That second voyage to Italy in 1846 was certainly very fortuitous for Newman, for, not only did he become friends with Giovanni Perrone, he also became much more familiar with St. Philip Neri and the Oratory that Neri had instituted. Newman's discovery of Neri would create a unique combination—a nineteenth-century Englishman and a sixteenth-century Italian. Together, they made each other known and respected throughout the world. As Father Antrobus explained in his 1902 introduction to Bacci's biography of Neri: "In conclusion, this New Edition of the Life of St. Philip, it is hoped, may prove acceptable to the many in England, and English-speaking countries, to whom his memory and virtues have become as household words, and who have felt the influence of the teaching and life of the Saint reproduced in our time in the lives and writings of two of St. Philip's most gifted sons, John Henry, Cardinal Newman, and Father Wilfrid Faber." [35]

Even though the writings of Faber and Newman helped to make Neri famous in England, St. Philip Neri was already widely revered in Italy. Born in Florence in 1515, Neri spent his younger years there studying with the Dominicans. At the age of 18, he went to Rome and continued to study philosophy and

[35] Frederick Ignatius Antrobus, preface to Father P. G. Bacci's *The Life of Saint Philip Neri* (London: Kegan Paul, Trench, Trubner, 1902), 1:xiii–xiv.

theology. In 1537, he completed his studies, sold his books, and gave himself solely to prayer. He began to frequent public places so that he could convert sinners. According to Bacci, "A little before the feast of Pentecost 1544 just before completing his 29th year, he received the miraculous gift of the Holy Ghost and the palpitation of his heart." [36]

Neri was ordained a priest in 1551, and he then began his apostolate of the confessional in which he encouraged his penitents to go to confession, to come back immediately if they should fall into sin, and above all else, to return to make frequent confessions.

> But from these meetings in the sacrament of confession there also grew up—as if of itself—Philip's proper and original creation: the Oratory. Philip knew that many sins had their source in the idleness and pleasure-seeking life of the day. And since many of his penitents went back after their confessions to wander through the streets, the idea came to him of keeping the band of young men together and simply keeping them busy. Automatically, meetings developed with a kind of spiritual conversation, which in essence were a continuation and summarizing of confession. The things for which there was no time in the individual confessions were discussed by Philip in his room in the afternoon. And to keep the little group together, there grew up in a natural and, one can even say, improvised way, the exercises that became typical of the Oratory. As evening drew on, they went out to one of the Seven Churches, or to Vespers with the Dominicans at the Minerva, or to hear a famous preacher. [37]

Philip and his group of men were to go through several trials and attacks as they grew in numbers, but, gradually, Philip saw his plans becoming more and more firmly established. He was too humble a man to have the boldness to found a congregation, yet he realized the wisdom of securing a place of his own where he could carry out the work that he had begun.

---

[36] Ibid., xx–xxi.
[37] Paul Turks, *Philip Neri: The Fire of Joy*, trans. Daniel Utrecht (New York: Alba House, 1995), 35–36.

While he was deliberating about this matter, two churches were proposed to him; Santa Maria in Monticelli, near the Strada della Regola, which was the easier to obtain, and Santa Maria in Vallicella in the Contrada di Parione, at that time a parish church. Being in doubt which of the two to take, he thought it would be well in a matter of such importance on which the fruit of the institute depended, to have a conference with the Pope, at that time Gregory XIII, considering this the best way to ascertain the will of God. The Pope recommended him to take the church of Santa Maria in Vallicella, as being in a more frequented part of the town than the other, and therefore best suited for the exercises. Philip received this answer as the expression of the will of God, and without any further delay took means to obtain the church.[38]

Thus, in September of 1575, the first stone was laid for the new church of Santa Maria in Vallicella where St. Philip would live and minister to the people of Rome until his death in 1595. "When Philip died, there were seven Oratories: in Rome, Naples, San Severino, Lucca, Fermo, Palermo, and Camerino. As the Constitutions of the Oratory still put it, these Congregations were founded *ad instar*, that is, on the model of the Roman house. One observed the life of the Roman house, the customary usages, how the authentic Oratory exercises were arranged and followed them. In fact, many of these early foundations came about through the personal influence of a member of the Roman house." [39] Thus, Philip's followers would continue his dream and his work so that his name would become legendary throughout Italy. Blessed Philip was canonized by Pope Gregory XV on 12 March 1622.[40]

In fact, there is evidence that John Henry Newman was aware of St. Philip Neri and his work even before he came to Rome in 1846. In a letter to F. W. Faber from Littlemore he said, "I have long felt special reverence and admiration for the character of St. Philip Neri, as far as I knew it, and was struck by

---

[38] Bacci, *The Life of Saint Philip Neri*, 1:105–106.
[39] Turks, *Philip Neri*, 144.
[40] Bacci, *The Life of Saint Philip Neri*, xxvi.

your saying that his church at Rome was in Vallicella—I wish
we could all become good Oratorians, but that, I suppose, is
impossible." [41] And in a note to that letter, Father Charles
Dessain explained that "the plan of joining the Oratory, hinted
at by Wiseman, was discussed at Littlemore, and Newman
procured a copy of the Rule of St. Philip, published by Abra-
ham Woodhead of University College in 1687." [42]

But, despite the urging of Wiseman, Newman himself was to
make the final choice in his search of a priestly vocation, and he
needed to do this in Italy. As he explained in his "Oratory
Papers":

> When I got to Rome, my first (and very crude) thought was
> to form and devote myself to the establishment of a theologi-
> cal college in England of secular priests. Then I said, "Shall
> I be a Jesuit?" And I mentioned the idea to my friends out of
> Rome as to Stanton, Dalgairns, A. Christie, etc., and then,
> after other inquiries and speculations, I said (in words which
> I have elsewhere used, perhaps in my address to the
> Wilfridians on admitting them into the Oratory on 14 Feb-
> ruary 1848). "Dear me! I have forgotten St. Philip," and then
> at once I began acquaintance with him, finding out his
> Church as the first step. . . . In a sense then that I could not
> say for certain that I should *not* be a Jesuit, I certainly ap-
> proximated to them about Christmas, 1846–7, but in the
> same sense I approximated to the Vincentians or Lazarists,
> to the Dominicans, to the Rosminians, and to others. . . .
> This interval, my first months at Rome, was devoted to a
> survey of the various religious bodies, there to be found, with
> reference not to my own vocation solely, but for one com-
> mon vocation, if possible, for me and the friends I had left
> behind me. [43]

Newman truly pursued in earnest to begin an "acquaintance"
with St. Philip. He arrived in Rome on Wednesday, 28 October
1846, and by November 6, he commented, "We have just been
to St. Philip Neri's Church (the Chiesa Nuova) where his relics

[41] Newman, "To F. W. Faber," *Letters and Diaries*, 11:105.
[42] Charles Dessain, in *Letters and Diaries*, 11:105.
[43] "Oratory Papers No. 36," in *Newman the Oratorian*, ed. Placid Murray, O.S.B.
(Dublin: Gill and Macmillan, 1969), 390–391.

lie—but only for a minute. I don't know how we are to see anything, what with three Lectures and Italian." [44] But despite his busy schedule, Newman continued to visit the Oratorians, and he was especially encouraged by Father Augustine Theiner, a German Oratorian who had come to Rome in 1839. By the end of December, Newman seemed to have made up his mind.

> We have seen the Chiesa Nuova (St. Philip's Church) and the Casa adjoining with Theiner—who said Mass with and for us and communicated us in the small room where St. Philip had his ecstacies. The Casa is the most beautiful thing of the kind we have seen in Rome—rather too comfortable, i.e., fine galleries for walking in summer, splendid orange trees, etc., etc. If I wished to follow my bent, I should join them, if I joined any—They have a good library and handsome sets of rooms apparently. It is like a College with hardly any rule. They keep their own property and furnish their own rooms. It is what Dr. Wiseman actually wishes, and really I should not wonder, if at last I felt strongly inclined to it, for I must own I feel the notion of giving up property tries my faith very much. [45]

When Newman had definitely made his decision, he formally asked the Pope for permission to erect an Oratory in Birmingham, England, as well as in other cities. He also asked to be allowed to adapt the Constitutions of the Roman Oratory to those that he would begin back home. "This version of the Constitutions was printed in Rome in 1847. Towards the end of this year, Newman and six companions began a noviciate in the Abbey of Santa Croce, an entire wing of which had been put at their disposal. For four months, they studied the Constitutions and customs of the Oratory, Newman working above all with the great biographies of St. Philip, Marciano's *History of the Oratory*, and the *Pregi* (*Excellences of the Oratory*)." [46]

Newman was overjoyed that he and his friends had been mandated to introduce the Oratory of St. Philip Neri into England,

---

[44] Newman, "To Richard Stanton," *Letters and Diaries*, 11:270.
[45] Newman, "To J. D. Dalgairns," *Letters and Diaries*, 11:303.
[46] Turks, *Philip Neri*, 149.

yet he was aware that they would have a formidable task. As he expressed his feelings to Lord Acton in February, 1847, "The Cardinal Prefect [of Propaganda, Fransoni] has shown himself most favorable, and the matter has since been brought before His Holiness, who has condescended to express his great approbation of it. He has even approved our sending for others of our friends from England and is desirous of removing all difficulties in the way of our carrying home with us the Tradition of St. Philip." [47]

There were many aspects of the Tradition of St. Philip that were so attractive to Newman that he wanted to take them from Italy back to his home. Generally speaking, he had a comfortable feeling about the Oratory system. As Bouyer said, "Cardinal Newman's motto, *Cor ad cor loquitur*, sums up the Philippian ideal; neither speeches nor arguments can awaken a living faith in those for whom Christianity has lost its meaning. Only contact with people whose daily lives are dominated by an intense and personal experience of the truths of the Faith can achieve such a result, and it is precisely this result which Philip achieved through his dual life of intimate communion with God and men." [48]

Specifically, Newman also perceived St. Philip Neri as a great example of a transmitter of Catholic Tradition. As has been discussed, for Newman, Tradition was movement—the divine doctrine passing from mouth to mouth, from father to son, from century to century. Tradition was "change and transformation in the sense of an organic, spiritual growth." [49] Dean Church, one of Newman's closest friends, offered an explanation for Newman's attraction to Neri: "In S. Filippo Neri, he could find a link between the New Testament and the modern world. He could find no San Filippo—so modern and yet so scriptural—when he sought at home." [50]

---

[47] Newman, "To Lord Acton," *Letters and Diaries*, 12:28.

[48] Louis Bouyer, *St. Philip Neri: A Portrait*, trans. Michael Day (London: Geoffrey Chapman, 1958), 72.

[49] Biemer, *Newman on Tradition*, 143.

[50] R. W. Church, quoted in C. S. Dessain, "Cardinal Newman's Attraction to St. Philip," *Oratorium* (1970), 71.

According to Father Dessain, Newman found in the Italian saint "a holiness adapted to the modern age, our age, something that could be really and genuinely put into practice, not an artificial imitation of the piety of past ages—and yet it must be the holiness of the New Testament, something all-absorbing and leading on through detachment to complete surrender to God. Newman thought he found all this in Saint Philip." [51]

Secondly, Newman was "quite won over by the character of Saint Philip—nature and grace, as always, inextricably intertwined." [52] In a letter to his sister in January of 1847, Newman tried to explain his attraction to the personality of St. Philip, while, at the same time, he discussed Manzoni's *I Promessi Sposi*. Newman was inundating Jemima, who was not even a Catholic, with a description of his favorite Italian saint and a reference to his favorite Italian novel:

> This great Saint reminds me in so many ways of Keble, that I can fancy what Keble would have been, if God's will had been he should have been born in another place and age; he was formed on the same type of extreme hatred of humbug, playfulness, nay oddity, tender love for others, and severity, which are the lineaments of Keble. From a child, he [Neri] was given up to religion, and though he enjoined no austerities in his Congregation or next to none, he went through almost incredible fasts and mortifications in his own person. His principle was that denial of the will was far more difficult than any mortification of body, and Theiner, who is now one of his Congregation. . . told us that, before he joined the Oratorians, he saw a good deal both of the Capuchins and Jesuits, but he found nowhere such real mortification as in the present successors of St. Philip. The Capuchins are the order to which Fra Christoforo belongs in the *Promessi Sposi*. They keep up the reputation which they had in the 16th century; they have indeed the greatest reputation in Rome. Men of noble birth and wealth give up everything and join them, and they do a great deal of good among the poor. [53]

---

[51] Ibid., 72.
[52] Ibid., 73.
[53] Newman, "To Mrs. John Mozley," *Letters and Diaries*, 12:23.

However, even though Newman greatly admired Manzoni's Fra Christoforo and the Capuchins, when he had to make the choice of a religious institute, he was more drawn to the system of St. Philip Neri. "In opting for the Oratory in preference to all other congregations, he gave himself up to a religious tradition which did not stifle his spirituality but allowed it to grow in a way that conformed to his tastes and provided a balanced way which most faithfully expressed his own ideal of truth and of evangelical simplicity." [54]

Further, Newman was drawn to the simplicity of the Oratory system because he felt, in some sense, that it was a return to the very first form of Christianity, as it existed in the lifetime of the Apostles. As he explained in his *Oratory Papers*:

> It was then a very bold and original undertaking on the part of St. Philip, more original perhaps than anything in the Rule of St. Ignatius. Primitive Christianity had been without decrees of faith, a rule of life, and rites for worship; I don't mean that Christianity ever was without a creed, a decalogue, or a sacrificial rite, but that there was a plainness and simplicity in the external laws of the primitive Church, whether as to doctrine, ethics or worship, peculiar to itself. . . . And what the Oratories were in worship, such were they still more strikingly in social converse—instead of vows or forcible impositions, they held it was enough to have Christian love, and they cultivated that love, towards God and man and each other, in the spirit of that great Apostle to whose inspired writings St. Philip had so special a devotion. [55]

The Italian Oratorians are very proud of the fact that John Henry Newman found in their beloved saint the structure and direction for the rest of his life, and they like to highlight the uniqueness of Neri that so appealed to Newman. For them, he had a charm that could only be found in an Italian. "But there is another aspect, I think, that above all else attracted Newman and gathers into a harmonious synthesis the entire interior life of Father Philip: It is that first verse of the very famous poem-prayer that in Italian we call *Guidami, luce gentile* ["Lead, Kindly Light"]. The 'gentleness' of Father Philip is much more than a mere character trait—it encompasses a sea of truth!" [56]

Newman tried never to forget the "gentilezza" of St. Philip Neri, for he knew that such a characteristic would be a useful one to teach to Oratorians who were "free subjects, who had few rules and must learn to live together by means of tact, self-knowledge, and the knowledge of others." [57] And, although the Oratory was to become his chosen vocation, and to found it in England was the first commission that he received from the Catholic authorities, Newman would need "gentilezza" to overcome some of the trials that he encountered as the English founder: [58]

> He was appointed Superior of the first foundation, which was to be in Birmingham, where Wiseman was Vicar Apostolic. This first house was set up at Old Oscott, rechristened Maryvale, on 1 February 1848, the eve of the Purification, which was the feast of St. Mary's College, Oriel, at Oxford. Shortly afterwards, at Wiseman's wish, and against his own judgment, Newman admitted as novices to the Oratory another convert group, headed by the emotional and exuberant Frederick William Faber. Early in 1849, Newman moved to Alcester Street in the middle of Birmingham, where the Oratory and a church were established with a parish and schools. He devoted himself to work among the poor, who included many with practically no knowledge of the Christian Faith, and many immigrants, Irish men and women driven to England by the Famine. In April he founded a second house of the Oratory in London, putting Faber in charge. . . . He only succeeded in founding two Oratories, although he had hoped for many more. Faber

[56] Edoardo Aldo Cerrato, "Saluto da Parte della Confederazione dell'Oratorio di San Filippo Neri," in *Conoscere Newman* (Città del Vaticano: Urbaniana University Press, 2002), 221.

[57] Charles Stephen Dessain, *John Henry Newman* (Stanford, Calif.: Stanford University Press, 1971), 92.

[58] Ibid., 93.

took with him to London Newman's prestige, but, especially after the London house became independent in 1853, it developed on different lines.[59]

This separation was difficult for Newman, for he never thought that he would suffer at the hands of some of his Oratorians. However, despite this disappointment, he was never to lose his love for St. Philip Neri and his Oratory system, and throughout the remainder of his life, Newman would include Neri in many of his writings. In *The Idea of a University*, his 1852 treatise on the importance of religion in education and on the hope for a Catholic university in Ireland, Newman discussed the lessons which he had gained from the history of his "own special Father and Patron, St. Philip Neri": [60]

> For me, if it be God's blessed will that in the years now coming I am to have a share in the great undertaking, which has been the occasion and the subject of these Discourses, so far I can say for certain that, whether or not I can do anything at all in St. Philip's way, at least I can do nothing in any other. Neither by my habits of life, nor by vigour of age, am I fitted for the task of authority, or of rule, or of initiation. I do not aspire, if strength is given me, to be your minister in a work which must employ younger minds and stronger lives than mine. I am but fit to bear my witness, to proffer my suggestions, to express my sentiments, as has in fact been my occupation in these discussions; to throw such light upon general questions, upon the choice of objects, upon the import of principles, upon the tendency of measures, as past reflection and experience enable me to contribute. I shall have to make appeals to your consideration, your friendliness, your confidence, of which I have had so many instances, on which I so tranquilly repose; and after all, neither you nor I must ever be surprised, should it so happen that the Hand of Him, with Whom are the springs of life and death, weighs heavy on me, and makes me unequal to anticipations in which you have been too kind, and to hopes in which I may have been too sanguine.[61]

[59] Ibid., 92–93.

[60] Newman, *The Idea of a University: Defined and Illustrated* (London: Longmans, Green and Co., 1927), 235.

[61] Ibid., 238–239.

Truly, the way of St. Philip Neri was leading Newman onward. And, later on in his life, when he published *Verses on Various Occasions,* five of the poems included were about St. Philip. Even though Newman's youthful enthusiasm had definitely diminished, his burden was being eased by the Italian saint:

> *So now, with his help, no cross will I fear,*
> *But will linger resign'd through my pilgrimage here,*
> *A child of St. Philip, my master and guide,*
> *I will live as he lived, and will die as he died.* [62]

---

[62] Newman, *Verses on Various Occasions* (London: Burns and Oates, 1883), 310.

VII

THE LATER YEARS AND
ITALIAN CATHOLIC TRADITION

Newman's Third Voyage to Italy (1856)

In 1856, John Henry Newman had been a Catholic for over ten years, he had studied in Rome and been ordained a priest, and he had instituted the two Oratories in England. However, difficulties lay ahead for Newman, and he would, once again, need inspiration from the memory of his patron saint and guidance from the Italian Oratories and the Pope. Newman himself must have been very disturbed with the happenings at this time in his life, for he wrote very little about them. But, the outstanding facts demonstrate that he, once again, turned to Italy and the Italians to help clarify the situation for him.

According to Wilfred Ward, the London Oratorians, under the leadership of Frederick W. Faber and without consulting Newman, had applied to the Office of Propaganda in Rome for permission to change their Rule so that they could be directors to religious communities:

> Propaganda appointed three Bishops to report on their application. At their recommendation, it granted the request, including the Birmingham community in the permission accorded. Newman was deeply pained at the transaction which had taken place without any previous communication with him—regarding it evidently as a symptom of a growing alienation from himself on the part of the London House. I am led to this conclusion because he shows, when referring to it in his letters, a feeling far deeper than the event by itself appears to warrant. It was probably the culminating point of a series of occurrences which had already caused him great pain. He tried to induce the London Oratorians to join him in applying to Rome for a distinct recognition of the inde-

pendence of each of the Houses. On their refusal to do so, he went to Rome himself, early in 1856, to place his views before the authorities. So deeply did he feel the importance of this appeal to the Holy See that on alighting from the *Diligence* he walked barefoot to St. Peter's to pray there before going to his hotel. He found on inquiry that the Holy Father had declined to confirm the decision of Propaganda until Newman himself should have been consulted.[1]

There can be no doubt that Newman was greatly upset about the friction between the two English Oratories. On December 27, he and St. John crossed to Calais en route to Rome. However, Newman felt the need to visit several northern Italian Oratories, before he was ready to tackle Rome and the Pope. Newman was very concerned about the future independence of his own Oratory, and he wanted to see how the Italians handled such a problem. His letters during this investigatory journey were very informative and complimentary of the aid that he was given.

From Turin he wrote:

> When we were introduced to the Father Superior of the Oratory of Turin, in the presence of the Padre Curato, who helped us on with him, he being so old, we first asked him whether in the Sardinian territories there had been or was danger of one Oratory exerting an undue influence, by whatever means, over another. He said it was impossible, for each ruled itself. We said but what if the Congregation of Bishops and Regulars or Propaganda were to interpret the Rule for the Oratory of Genoa, would not that affect Turin? He said, "Not at all—for the Father Superior and Deputies interpret the Rule for themselves, and any interpretation for another House does not affect them."[2]

Newman and St. John continued onward asking to have a meeting at the Verona Oratory. As Newman explained to the Provost in his less than perfect Italian —"We would also like to request from your kindness in the name of the Congregation of

---

[1] Wilfred Ward, *The Life of John Henry Cardinal Newman* (London: Longmans, Green, and Co., 1912), 1:450–451.

[2] Newman "To Nicholas Darnell," *Letters and Diaries*, 17:106–107.

Birmingham, that we could ask you some questions about the Rule of Saint Philip." [3] The Provost agreed to the meeting with the two Englishmen, and he corroborated what they had learned in Turin. "In answer to our questions, he said (in the presence of four to six other Fathers, who sometimes joined in the conversation), that he did not conceive any Brief necessary for establishing a House, nor that one House had any power of propagating others." [4]

The men continued onward, making their way through northern Italy as they visited Oratories along the way. They learned much from this experience—information that would help them with their immediate problem with the London Oratory and would give them future guidance on how to conduct their Oratory. They found that it was generally agreed that an application to Rome from one Oratory for a particular dispensation from the Rule of St. Philip would not impose any obligation on another Oratory, and that the spiritual direction for nuns was possible, but not usual. "Newman did not know about the London Oratory's circular letter, but the replies from the Provosts of the Oratories Newman had visited assured Faber that Newman's only object seemed to be to safeguard the individual autonomy of the English Oratories, and that his only concern was that Rome in its dealings with one Oratory would not bind or compromise another." [5]

Therefore, the Italian Oratorians helped to reassure both Newman and Faber that neither had compromised the integrity of his own Oratory. However, Newman still felt that he had to continue on to Rome so that he could clear his name with both the Office of Propaganda and the Pope. On 25 January 1856, Newman and St. John had an audience with Pius IX, who had on his desk the London Oratory's report to Propaganda, accusing Newman of trying to make himself "general" of the English Oratories. "St. John, whose Italian was better than

---

[3] Newman, "To Carlo Zamboni, Provost of the Oratory at Verona," *Letters and Diaries*, 17:108.

[4] Newman, "To Nicholas Darnell," *Letters and Diaries*, 17:110.

[5] Ian Ker, *John Henry Newman: A Biography* (Oxford University Press, 1988), 427.

Newman's, understood the Pope to say hurriedly at the beginning that he had heard Newman had come to make himself head of the English Congregation of the Oratory. However, the audience went off well, and St. John was able to give their version of the affair, which the Pope seemed to accept. The Pope even remarked that he did not want them to occupy themselves with nuns." [6]

Newman was very satisfied with their meeting with the Pope. As he described it to Edward Caswell:

We have just had a long and most satisfactory interview with the Pope—and I can say that it is well we have come here. He knew all about *us*, down to Father Dalgairns, and wished evidently to *hear our side*, having heard the other. . . . The Pope appointed us in the kindest way to see us by ourselves; we were with him from three quarters of an hour to an hour. He began by saying I was thin and had done much penance—and that Father Ambrose had got older. We began by thanking him for his many favors, which pleased him. . . . The Pope now said that he had an image of St. Philip, given him by an old priest, no great thing, but dear from memory—he had had it over his bed for eighteen years. He said he would give it to me and went to fetch it. . . . Father Ambrose had said that we have come to see various Oratories and especially Chiesa Nuova, and to learn most exactly the traditions of the Oratory. . . . Ambrose went on to recount what we did at Birmingham—a large parish—a poor house with hospital (he said, "Good, good") a jail—schools, etc. (He said, "*Tutto eccellente*") and that nuns did not suit us—and that what suited one Oratory need not suit another—and that all we wanted was that each Oratory should do its own work. He said "*Ne penserò io*." "I will see to that." . . . Then we moved; kissed his ring, received his blessing, and then asked his blessing on the Congregation—which he gave solemnly—blessing *patres et fratres totius congregationis*. [7]

The result of the audience with the Pope was that Monsignor Alessandro Barnabò, the Secretary to the Roman Congregation of Propaganda, was far more gracious to Newman, and

[6] Ibid., 428.
[7] Newman, "To Edward Caswell," *Letters and Diaries*, 17:135–138.

he advised Newman to refrain from petitioning the Pope "that nothing done by the Holy See by one Oratory might affect another." Barnabò said that the grant of it would diminish Newman's power as *Deputato Apostolico* for setting up an Oratory in any part of England. After this meeting with Barnabò, Newman was happy to withdraw the proposal that had provided the basis for the accusation that he wanted control over all the English Oratories.[8] Newman was happy with the outcome. "Everything is turning out well—and I can never feel anything but thankfulness and satisfaction that I have come here."[9]

Thus, Newman's third trip to Italy was a very enlightening one for him and for the Birmingham Oratory. He and St. John had learned "most exactly the tradition of the Oratory" from the Italians, and they had cleared their name and garnered further direction from both the Pope and the Office of Propaganda. The Pope had even given him an image of St. Philip! Early in February, they took a Neapolitan steamer for Marseilles, traveled through France, and arrived in Birmingham ready to return to work. As Newman summed up the experience to Cardinal Wiseman:

> Your Eminence will be pleased to know that my mission has been entirely successful. Before I started, I told our Fathers that I should make it my rule not to say one word in complaint or adversion against the London House. I am glad to say that I have succeeded both for ourselves, and without introducing them; except that I have brought the Pope's blessing, which I asked for them. He has been most exceedingly kind and careful about us—and knows more of the Birmingham House than he did before.[10]

Yet, there was one disappointment that Newman expressed about this trip to Italy. When he and St. John had their meeting with the Pope, Newman had to allow St. John to do the explaining to the Pontiff, and Newman could not understand everything that the Pope had said. Newman regretted that his Italian

---

[8] See Ker, *John Henry Newman*, 428.
[9] Newman: quoted in ibid.
[10] Newman, "To Cardinal Wiseman," *Letters and Diaries*, 17:144.

was not better—"I only wish my knowledge of Italian was sufficient to have followed him [the Pope] as minutely." [11]

The Remembrance of Italian Friends during the Difficult Years

As the years went by, Newman did not significantly increase his understanding of the Italian language, but he was never to forget the Italians who had embraced him as a Catholic and who had helped him to understand Catholic Tradition. Pope Pius IX had given him an image of St. Philip Neri, and Newman was always to keep both the image and the inspiration of St. Philip close to his heart.

In fact, Newman seemed to gain great solace from the Italian saint, and he mentioned him often during the traumatic times after his return from Rome in 1856. Newman was now in his late fifties, and events were turning against him:

> His fateful involvement in the affairs of the liberal Catholic *Rambler* that led to his publishing what is one of his most famous theological writings, his lengthy article "On Consulting the Faithful in Matters of Doctrine" (1859), had resulted in his falling under the suspicion and disapproval of the ecclesiastical authorities in Rome as well as England. His first real experience of the authoritarian clericalism of the nineteenth-century Catholic Church had come with his disappointing and frustrating association with the ill-fated Catholic University of Ireland which he had struggled to launch as its first president (1851–8). It seemed not only to him but to most Catholics who counted that he had nothing more to contribute and that he was lucky to have avoided a formal censure for the offending article. The Oratory he had founded in Birmingham in 1848 was hardly thriving: in fact, it was so depleted that much of the community and pastoral work now had to be done by Newman himself. The daughter house that had been founded in London under the flamboyant Father (F. W.) Faber was not only much better known and successful but was in active opposition both to

[11] Newman, "To Edward Caswell," *Letters and Diaries,* 17:136.

Newman's idea of the nature of an Oratory and to the kind of moderate Catholicism he was trying to promote in an increasingly polarized church.[12]

Newman's *Letters and Diaries* during those difficulties indicate how much he turned to St. Philip. In Volumes XVIII and XIX—a period from April 1857 to June 1861—Newman mentioned him more than forty times. At one point he said: "I could not leave the world with a good conscience, if I had not given my last years to St. Philip."[13] And later that year, he told Henry Wilburforce, "And, I, like Job, have friends, Baldads, and Sophars, who lament so very much, that I am so given up by God and St. Philip."[14]

Although Newman considered his allegiance to St. Philip second only to his allegiance to God, he, likewise, never forgot his other Italian friends. In the 1850s and 1860s, his letters contain numerous references to St. Alphonsus Liguori, Blessed Dominic Barberi, and Father Giovanni Perrone. Newman also worried about the problems facing Italian religious houses when laws were being enforced against them by the Piedmont government. He said, "As to Italy, its state is wretched. We must all feel intensely for the Holy Fathers, and for the poor nuns who are driven out of their convents, and for St. Philip's Houses, which I fear are to suffer—but, as to Italy in its length and breadth, it does what it does *con amore*—and it is likely to reap as it has sown."[15]

More problems were arising for Newman as they were for Italy. At the beginning of 1864, he appeared to be a neglected, powerless man. In addition, Charles Kingsley, a well-known novelist and professor, wrote a book review for *Macmillan's Magazine* in which he mentioned that Father Newman believed that truth for its own sake was not a necessary virtue for Roman clergy. After an acrimonious exchange between the two men,

---

[12] Ian Ker, Introduction, in *Apologia*, xv.
[13] Newman, "To Ambrose St. John," *Letters and Diaries*, 18:33.
[14] Newman, "To Henry Wilberforce," *Letters and Diaries*, 18:267.
[15] Newman, "To Miss M. R. Giberne," *Letters and Diaries*, 19:476.

"Newman decided that there was only one charge against him, that of untruthfulness, and it was accepted by many in England who thought he had led a secret Catholic movement to undermine the Church of England, while still a member of it. This imputation had lain on him for twenty years, and now he had the opportunity to remove it." [16]

"The result was the *Apologia,* which appeared in weekly parts from April to June 1864." [17] There are many reasons why the *Apologia* has been considered one of the greatest spiritual memoirs of all time, but one interesting feature of the work is the appreciation that Newman expressed for Italy and the individual Italians who had helped him understand Catholic Tradition. As he said about his first trip to Italy: "I was not ungrateful for the comfort which I had received in frequenting the churches; nor did I ever forget it. Then again, her zealous maintenance of the doctrine and the rule of celibacy, which I recognized as Apostolic, and her faithful agreement with Antiquity in so many other points which were dear to me, was an argument as well as a plea in favor of the great Church of Rome." [18] In addition, Newman mentioned his Sicilian servant, Gennaro, St. Alfonso, and, of course, his beloved St. Philip Neri. He even closed the history of himself "with St. Philip's name upon St. Philip's feast-day," [19] on 26 May 1864.

That day was a fortuitous one for Newman. As Father Bouyer has described it, the cloud was lifted:

> The publication of the *Apologia,* and the warmth of its reception, began to bring about a change in Newman's position. It looked as if the dawn was breaking. The uncomprehending attitude of Protestants, and, what was still worse, of Catholics, was not dispelled all at once. But the tide began to turn in his favor, and slowly and surely, pursued its course. Not only was the ever-growing neglect he had suffered at last made up for, but it soon became clear that in him the

[16] Dessain, *John Henry Newman,* 122.
[17] Ibid.
[18] *Apologia,* 65.
[19] Ibid., 250.

Church had one of the most gifted of her children, and perhaps, one of the most saintly.[20]

Newman's struggles were not over, but he seemed to gain more confidence in his position as a Catholic priest and spiritual leader. Thus, he had the courage to defend the theological credibility of St. Alfonso Liguori against an Anglican friend who went "somewhat too far in what he says in depreciation of St. Alfonso's importance."[21] In addition, when another friend, Dr. Russell of Maynooth wanted him "to withdraw the statement that the Pope in ecumenical council was the normal seat of infallibility, or to hesitate in his conviction that certain Italian devotions to Our Lady were not suitable for England, he refused absolutely."[22] And, as the years progressed, John Henry Newman never forgot what he had learned in Italy and the Italians who had taught him.

Cardinal Newman's Final Trip to Rome

By October 1867, Newman was finally beginning to feel an intensification of the inward peace that had been his since he became a Catholic.[23] As he wrote in his diary:

> I was never in such happy circumstances as now, and I do not know how I can fancy I shall continue without some or other real cross. I am my own master—I have my time my own—I am surrounded with comforts and conveniences—I am in easy circumstances, I have no cares, I have good health—I have no pain of mind or body. I enjoy life too well. The weight of the years falls on me as snow, gently though surely, but I do not feel it yet. I am surrounded with dear friends—my reputation has been cleared by the *Apologia*. . . . I am covered with blessings, and as full of God's gifts as is conceivable. And I have nothing to ask for but pardon and grace, and a happy death.[24]

[20] Louis Bouyer, *St. Philip Neri: A Portrait*, trans. Michael Day (London: Geoffrey Chapman, 1958), 363.

[21] Newman, "To Lady Chatterton," *Letters and Diaries*, 21:139.

[22] Ian Ker, Introduction, in *Letters and Diaries*, 21:xiv.

[23] See J. Lewis May, *Cardinal Newman* (Westminster, Md.: The Newman Press, 1951), 240.

[24] Newman, quoted in ibid. (unverified).

However, God was not yet ready for Newman, and there would be further challenges ahead. Once again, Newman was busy writing. In 1866, in his "Letter Addressed to the Rev. Edward B. Pusey, D.D., on the Occasion of His *Eirenicon*," Newman spoke of the connection between his Catholic idea of Scripture and Tradition and that of Pusey, his Anglican friend. According to Biemer, this topic was not a new one. "As might have been expected, Newman simply offers here the converse of his argument from the *Essay on Development*. He had then recognized, at the end of his years as an Anglican, that his previous notions on Scripture and Tradition were perfectly compatible with those of the Council of Trent. And now, speaking as a Catholic to his Anglican colleague, he affirms that the difference between the two views is ultimately simply verbal." [25]

According to Newman, both Catholicism and Anglicanism insisted that the teachings of Tradition must be taken into account in the interpretation of Scripture. However, most Anglicans minimized the importance of Tradition in the transmission of faith. Dessain summarized Newman's view:

> Catholics said that not every article of faith was so contained in Scripture "that it may thence be logically proved, *independently* of the teaching and authority of Tradition," Anglicans that every article of faith was contained in Scripture, "provided there be added the illustrations and compensations supplied by the *Tradition*," Anglicans did not say "that the whole revelation is in Scripture, in such sense that pure unaided logic can draw it from the sacred text," nor did Catholics say "that it was not in Scripture, in an improper sense, in the sense that the *Tradition* of the Church is able to recognize and determine it there." [26]

Therefore, Newman explained to Pusey that a Catholic tradition had to take into consideration the time and the place before any judgment could be made about its validity:

> And so, again certain statements may be true, under circumstances and in a particular time and place, which are

---

[25] Günter Biemer, *Newman on Tradition* (New York: Herder and Herder, 1967), 63.
[26] Dessain, *John Henry Newman*, 136.

abstractedly false; and hence it may be very unfair in a controversialist to interpret by an English or a modern rule, whatever may have been asserted by a foreign or medieval author. To say, for instance, dogmatically, that no one can be saved without personal devotion to the Blessed Virgin, would be an untenable proposition; yet it might be true of this man or that, or of this or that country at this or that date; and, if that very statement has ever been made by any writer of consideration (and this has to be ascertained), then perhaps it was made precisely under these exceptional circumstances. If an Italian preacher made it, I should feel no disposition to doubt him, at least if he spoke of Italian youths and Italian maidens.[27]

Thus, Newman used Italy as an example of a special consideration—a country in which the depth of spirituality could lead to a definition of Tradition which might include a different style of devotion from that practiced in England.

Continuing with his writing, early in 1870 Newman published *A Grammar of Assent*, which he had been trying to compose, making numerous drafts, for twenty years. In this work, "Newman wanted to find the answer to a crucial problem; he wished to justify men's right to be certain, and especially their right to certitude in matters of religion."[28] At the same time, Newman was asked to be a Consultor on one of the preparatory Commissions of the First Vatican Council. "He weighed up the pros and cons and decided he ought to decline. His work (he was then writing *A Grammar of Assent*) would be seriously interrupted, he had never succeeded in working on boards or committees, could not make his presence felt among high ecclesiastics, knew no language but his own, and his health was not good."[29]

Perhaps Newman was so loyal to his friends in both England and Italy because he was very modest and did not consider

---

[27] Newman, "A Letter addressed to the Rev. E. B. Pusey, D.D., on occasion of his *Eirenicon* of 1864," in *Certain Difficulties Felt by Anglicans in Catholic Teaching* (London: Basil Montagu Pickering, 1876), 104–105.

[28] Dessain, *John Henry Newman*, 148.

[29] Ibid., 137.

himself to be among the "high ecclesiastics," nor did he enjoy the status of clubs or committees. He seemed to be most happy corresponding with his numerous friends and acquaintances as they exchanged ideas and reflections. But, at this time in his life, unfortunately, Newman was beginning to lose some of those people who were dearest to him. Of course, the greatest blow of all was the death of his much beloved Ambrose St. John in the spring of 1875. After his death came others, and they deepened the sorrows of Newman's declining years:

> William Wilberforce went in the summer; so too did the faithful matron of the Oratory School, Mrs. Wootten. Father Caswall in the following year was pronounced by the doctors to be hopelessly ill. Others, once his friends, though now either long separated from him or estranged, passed away—as Richard Simpson and J. D. Dalgairns. Newman's letters dwell constantly on these losses. A new degree of sadness and solemnity is apparent in them, little relieved by brighter thoughts.[30]

By this time also, Newman had already lost most of his Italian friends—Barberi in 1849, Rosmini in 1855, and Manzoni in 1873. Father Giovanni Perrone was soon to follow in 1876. What he said about his English friends could also apply to his contemporary Italian friends—"Three have gone, the fourth is going. I trust they may do something for me according to God's Blessed Will in compensation for my bereavement in losing them. And when am I to join them? What a thick darkness is over the future!"[31]

Il Cardinale Enrico Newman

Little did Newman know that his future would not be "thick darkness," and that all of his deceased friends were "doing something" for him, for, certainly, they were praying. Toward the end of January 1879, Cardinal Lorenzo Nina, the Pope's

---

[30] Wilfred Ward, *Life of . . . Newman*, 2:413.
[31] Newman, "To Mother Mary Imelda Poole," *Letters and Diaries*, 28:154.

Secretary of State, wrote to Cardinal Manning in London, asking him to find out in strict confidence whether John Newman would accept a Cardinal's hat. Through Bishop Ullathorne of Birmingham, the news reached Newman on January 31, and, for the first time since the death of Ambrose St. John, Newman felt elation and vindication. However, another problem presented itself. "Although much moved by the Pope's kind action, there remained the difficulty that it was almost unheard of for a Cardinal who was not a diocesan bishop to live out of Rome. At his age, and with his Oratory full of new recruits needing his care, how could he leave Birmingham for Rome and the grandeur of a Prince of the Church?" [32]

The next month was one of great turmoil for Newman because he did not want to negotiate with the Pope, but he also knew that he was too old and tired to move to Italy. However, the matter was resolved by the end of February, and he finally received a copy of a letter from Cardinal Manning to Bishop Ullathorne which included the following good news: "The Holy Father gave me leave to write and say that Dr. Newman would not be required to change his way of life, or leave the Oratory, or come to Rome, and that letters in this sense will be written to him. Perhaps you will kindly make this known to Dr. Newman." [33]

Newman waited several more weeks, and then he himself got the formal announcement from Cardinal Nina. Newman was so delighted that he quoted the first line to several of his friends. "The Holy Father, greatly appreciating the brilliance, the doctrine that distinguishes your Most Reverend Priesthood, the piety, as well as your zeal, demonstrated in the exercise of the Sacred Ministry, the devotion and filial attachment to the Holy and Apostolic See. And the appointed services, that for so many years you have rendered to the Faith, has determined to give you a public and solemn proof of his esteem and benevo-

---

[32] Ian Ker, Introduction, *Letters and Diaries*, 29:xiii.

[33] Cardinal Henry Edward Manning, "To Bishop Ullathorne," *Letters and Diaries*, 29:48.

lence." [34] The Pope had recognized Newman's long years of devotion to the Catholic Church.

Despite the fact that Newman knew the voyage and the weather might be very detrimental to his health, he accepted the Pope's invitation to come to Rome to receive his Cardinal's hat. This decision was probably a two-fold one—first, Newman was so appreciative of the honor that Pope Leo had given him, and second, he seemed to have a longing to visit Italy once again before he died. He expressed these feelings to his friend, John O'Hagan:

> Of course, I view the wonderful change of things as you view it. It was the reason which when the Holy Father so considerately allowed me to live here, made me put away every other thought and constrained me to accept the honor. I felt that he was generously and tenderly clearing me from the charges which were made against me. I used to say to myself, "Time will set me right, I must be patient, for Time is on my side." But the Pope has superseded Time. How should I not be most grateful to him!
>
> I set off for Rome tomorrow, and ask you and Mrs. O'Hagan to say a good prayer for me, for I rather dread both the journey and the climate. [35]

Newman was right to "dread the journey and the climate." He left the Oratory for Rome on 16 April 1879, accompanied by Father William Neville, the priest who became his primary confidant after the death of St. John. And, of course, Newman caught a cold in Genoa. "Unable to take wine, the journey was too much for me, and I had to remain two days at Pisa—else, we should have been at Rome on Tuesday night—but we stayed an idle day at Pisa, and another day went no further than Siena—and so we got here by 4:30 P.M. yesterday, Thursday. . . . Everyone has been surpassingly kind. . . . I make a bad hand at Italian, the easiest of languages." [36]

By this, his last trip to Rome, Newman was again very upset

[34] Cardinal Lorenzo Nina, "To John Henry Newman," *Letters and Diaries*, 29:84.
[35] Newman, "To John O'Hagan," *Letters and Diaries*, 29:105–106.
[36] Newman, "To Arthur Wollaston Hutton," *Letters and Diaries*, 29:107.

that he had never quite mastered the ability to speak Italian. But despite this regret and his illness, he took a great deal of time to respond to William Froude about the importance of living the Catholic life in order to experience the promise of Revelation:

> You say, "The communication of mind with mind cannot be effected by any purely abstract process." I consider when I sum up the course of thought by which I am landed in Catholicity, that it consists in three propositions: that there has been or will be a Revelation; that Christianity is that Revelation; and that Catholicity is its legitimate expression; and that these propositions naturally strengthen the force of each. But this is only how I should sum up in order to give outstanders an idea of my line of argument, not as myself having been immediately convinced by abstract propositions. Nothing surely have I insisted on more earnestly in my *Essay on Assent*, than on the necessity of thoroughly subjecting abstract propositions to concrete. It is in the experience of daily life that the power of religion is learnt.... And I repeat, it is not by syllogisms or other logical process that trustworthy conclusions are drawn, such as command our assent, but by the minute, continuous, experimental reasoning, which shows badly on paper, but which drifts silently into an overwhelming cumulus of proof, and, when our start is true, brings us on to a true result.[37]

How appropriate that Newman should have written this explanation in Rome, for throughout his life as a Catholic, many of his experiences with Italian saints and theologians helped him to learn more about the Catholic religion. In fact, Newman became very defensive of the Italians when a German Liberal, Dr. Döllinger, commented that Newman was a man who was infinitely above the Romish *vulgus praelaticum*, and, further, the Pope had made him a Cardinal because the people in Rome did not know his true views. Döllinger added that if Newman had written in French, Italian, or Latin, his books would have long since been condemned. Newman replied, "Dr.

---

[37] Newman, "To William Froude," *Letters and Diaries*, 29:116.

Döllinger's declaration has pained me very much, as it displays an irritability and want of benevolence towards me which I did not expect from him. It is ridiculous to suppose that the Romans, of all the people in the world, would be wanting in acuteness, or that they are not people enough to accuse me of heterodoxy if they could do so." [38]

However, even though Newman had to face physical sickness and the Döllinger controversy, he was delighted when the Romans showed their love for him by enthusiastically welcoming him to their city. On Monday, 12 May 1879, Newman went to the Palazzo della Pigna, the residence of Cardinal Howard, of the English College. There Newman received the *biglietto* from the Cardinal Secretary of State informing him that at a Consistory that same morning the Pope had raised him to the rank of Cardinal. "By eleven o'clock, the room was crowded with English and American Catholics, ecclesiastics and laymen, as well as many members of the Roman nobility and dignitaries of the Church, assembled to witness the ceremony. Soon after midday, the consistorial messenger was announced. He handed the *biglietto* to Cardinal Newman, who, having broken the seal, gave it to Dr. Clifford, Bishop of Clifton, who read the contents." [39]

Newman paid the customary compliments and responded with his *biglietto* speech:

> Vi ringrazio, Monsignore, per la participazione che m'avete fatto dell'alto onore che il Santo Padre si è degnato conferire sulla mia umile persona [I thank you, Monsignor, for your participation in the high honor that the Holy Father has deigned to confer on my humble person].—And if I ask your permission to continue my address to you, not in your musical language, but in my own dear mother tongue, it is because in the latter I can better express my feelings on the most gracious announcement which you have brought to me than if I attempted what is above me.
>
> First of all, then, I am led to speak of the wonder and profound gratitude which came upon me, and which is upon

---

[38] Newman, "To an Unknown Correspondent," *Letters and Diaries*, 29:132.
[39] Wilfred Ward, *Life of . . . Newman*, 2:459.

me still, at the condescension and love towards me of the Holy Father, in singling me out for so immense an honor. It was a great surprise. Such an elevation had never come into my thoughts, and seemed to be out of keeping with all my antecedents. I had passed through many trials, but they were over; and now the end of all things had almost come to me, and I was at peace. And was it possible that after all I had lived through so many years for this? [40]

Newman continued by discussing the essence of his life's work:

... For thirty, forty, fifty years I have resisted to the best of my powers the spirit of Liberalism in religion. ... Liberalism in religion is the doctrine that there is no positive truth in religion, but that one creed is as good as another, and this is the teaching which is gaining substance and force daily. It is inconsistent with any recognition of any religion as *true*. It teaches that all are to be tolerated, for all are matters of opinion. Revealed religion is not a truth, but a sentiment and a taste; not an objective fact, not miraculous, and it is the right of each individual to make it say just what strikes his fancy. Devotion is not necessarily founded on faith. [41]

And the Italians responded with great aplomb to both Newman's ideas and his persona. In a letter to a friend at home, Father Pope recounted their reaction to the new English Cardinal: "All has passed off beautifully—an immense crowd—the Father made a very fine speech . . . which is very heartily enjoyed here. . . . How he managed it St. Philip knows best—but he did not cough—and his delivery was very animated, and perfect, as the vehicle of his words. . . . The Italian ladies behind me were unanimous that he was: 'che bel vecchio! Che figura!' etc., etc. 'Pallido sì, ma bellissimo!' [What a beautiful old man! What a figure! etc., etc. Pale, yes, but most beautiful.] In short, the Father was quite up to the occasion, which is saying a great deal!" [42]

[40] Newman, quoted in ibid.
[41] Ibid., 2:460.
[42] Father Thomas Pope, in ibid., 2:463.

Thus, the new seventy-eight-year-old Cardinal became quite popular among the women of Rome. But, unfortunately, he could not accomplish everything that he had wanted to do while in Italy. There were certain Italian friends whom he wanted to visit, including a priest at St. Catherine's in Bologna and the Archbishop of Turin, Lorenzo Gastaldi, a Rosminian.[43] And, of course, Newman wanted to spend time with St. Philip's Oratorians. All of these plans were cancelled. As he explained to the Duke of Norfolk:

> I have been strictly confined to my room and my bed. On Ascension Day [May 22] I was not even allowed to go into the next room to *hear* Mass, and tomorrow, alas, when the Pope wished me to be the great person at Chiesa Nuova, and all the poor Oratorians were cheering themselves in their misfortunes [the Italian Government had seized the larger part of the Roman Oratory] in the anticipation of welcoming an Oratorian Cardinal, I am forbidden to go out of this house under the threat that it might possibly be a case of life and death. . . .
>
> I cannot be in kinder hands. I am shocked at the prospect of disappointing warm-hearted people, who wish to see me.[44]

Therefore, after a final audience with the Pope on June 2, John Henry Newman left Rome for the last time. The Italians who had helped him understand Catholic Tradition were long since gone. But he still never failed to comment on the goodness of the people whom he had met on this last trip; as he wrote in one letter, "I could not have a better man than Giorgio, he has quite satisfied me."[45] From Gennaro in 1833 to Giorgio in 1879, Newman was certainly treated with loving care while in Italy, and he never forgot the kind ministrations of these men.

Likewise, Newman would mention for the rest of his life his Italian mentors, most especially, St. Philip Neri. Newman was seventy-eight years old when he was made a Cardinal, and he

[43] Newman, "To John Norris," *Letters and Diaries*, 29:125.
[44] Newman, "To the Duke of Norfolk," *Letters and Diaries*, 29:129–130.
[45] Ibid., 126.

would spend the last eleven years of his life in comparative peace, with his growing Oratory community, his school, his many visitors, and his correspondence.[46] Newman said his last Mass on Christmas Day of 1889. "He knew he was too infirm and blind to say it any longer with safety, though he continued to say a 'dry' Mass in the hope that it might become possible to celebrate once more. St. Philip said his last Mass on the feast of Corpus Christi, Newman at Christmas—'they are cognate feasts,' he said in 1847, celebrating his first Mass in England at Christmas, as his very first had been at Corpus Christi, in Rome." [47]

And, again, on 11 July 1890, in one of his last letters, Newman wrote to a priest friend and mentioned, with his usual great humility, both his beloved St. Philip and his beloved friends:

> I feel very grateful for your most tender care and thoughtfulness and affectionate attachment towards me as shown by the splendid spiritual bouquet you procured for me on St. Philip's Day, and I thank yourself and the contributors for so great a mercy with all my heart. I wish my want of power of showing my gratitude could be brought home to my many friends and true benefactors. You must, please, believe what I have not the opportunity or means of showing, and you will be too kind not to give me credit for it. You know, I am sure, how difficult it is for me to write or read and will excuse me.[48]

Cardinal John Henry Newman died on 11 August 1890, exactly one month after writing that poignant letter. He was buried in accordance with the instructions that he had left, in the grave of his most beloved friend, Ambrose St. John, and on the pall was his chosen motto, *Cor ad cor loquitur.* [49]

[46] See Dessain, *John Henry Newman*, 165.

[47] Meriol Trevor, *Newman's Journey* (Huntington, Ind.: Our Sunday Visitor, 1985), 254.

[48] Newman, "To John Thomas Walford, S.J.," *Letters and Diaries*, 31:297.

[49] Wilfred Ward, *Life of . . . Newman*, 2:537.

VIII

CONCLUSION

There can be no doubt that John Henry Newman learned many aspects of Catholic Tradition from his Italian friends. These people, two Italian saints and four contemporary Italians, provided him with an understanding of Catholicism that he could not seem to obtain from his own people and in his own country. As Ian Ker has said, "The story of John Henry Newman's conversion to Catholicism is not quite the same as the story of his discovery of Catholicism. . . . Now while Newman knew a very great deal about the early Church, he knew extraordinarily little about contemporary Catholicism, apart from its formal doctrines and teaching."[1]

In fact, on his first trip to Italy, Newman carried with him a prejudice against both Catholics and Italians. And yet, despite his determination to avoid Italians at all cost, he seemed to have been drawn to them and to their worship. When he left Italy after that voyage, he was changed forever. For in Italy, Newman made the discovery of a highly practical and useful kind of religion. Instead of something supernatural, far removed from the ordinary mundane world, Italian Catholicism was a much more spiritual religion that that of the Church of England, which seemed, paradoxically, a far more matter-of-fact kind of "business."[2]

This spiritual and all-encompassing religion was what Newman craved, and from that point on, the Catholicism of John Henry Newman and the Catholicism of St. Alfonso Liguori, Bl. Dominic Barberi, Alessandro Manzoni, Antonio Rosmini,

---

[1] Ian Ker, *The Catholic Revival in English Literature, 1845–1961* (Notre Dame, Ind.: University of Notre Dame Press, 2003), 13.
[2] Ibid., 20.

Giovanni Perrone, and St. Philip Neri would be forever intertwined. An Italian, Cardinal Capecelatro, best explained this
unique relationship when he gave a commemoration speech
shortly after the death of John Henry Newman. For Capecelatro and for the whole world, John Henry Newman was equally
English and Italian; the best of the English because by preserving the character and the exceptional prayers of his race, he was
able to spread among his people his new light of truth and of
love; the best of the Italian because by absorbing their stability
of belief and their Catholic traditions, he was able to combine a
loving intellect with a life of holiness:

> In sum, Newman has been at the same time English and
> Italian; an excellent Englishman, observing the character
> and rare qualities of his race, he has spread among his
> people a new light of truth and love; an excellent Italian
> because from the Vicar of Christ, who is in the midst of our
> Italy, he has drawn firmness of belief and likewise, with a
> loving intellect and with a life of holiness, has defended and
> reinvigorated among us as well that faith which conquers
> every error, that faith which is so sublime to us. Further-
> more, the learned and saintly English Oratorian has been
> Italian and one of us, also because, as all great Catholics, he
> had a particular love for Italy, from where all the peoples of
> Europe have drawn the benefit of Christianity that, thanks
> to the Vicar of Christ, that here in Italy unifies, that here
> teaches without the dangers of errors, that for centuries has
> been mirrored, more lively than anywhere else, in the life of
> thought, of the fine arts, and of civilization. If the same
> Christ, as the Divine Poet says, is Roman, it is therefore right
> that all the noble and strong imitators of Christ would also
> be Romans, and, for a reasonable extension of that name,
> would also be Italians. Therefore, my dearest children, let us
> consider Cardinal Newman to be one of us.[3]

Thus, with this love and support from his Italian friends,
John Henry Newman was able to live his motto—COR AD COR
LOQUITUR—until the day of his death.

---

[3] Cardinale Alfonso Capecelatro, "Commemorazione del Cardinale Enrico Newman," speech given to the Confratelli dell'Oratorio di Napoli, 6 November 1890
(Napoli: Tipografia dell'Accademia Reale delle Scienze, 1890), 4–5.

BIBLIOGRAPHY

PRIMARY SOURCES

Apologia pro Vita Sua: Being a History of His Religious Opinions, 1864. Reprint: edited by Ian Ker. London: Penguin Books, 1994.

The Arians of the Fourth Century, 1833. Reprint: Westminster, Md.: Christian Classics, Inc., 1968.

Autobiographical Writings. Edited by Henry Tristram. New York: Sheed & Ward, 1957.

Callista: A Sketch of the Third Century, 1855. Reprint: New York: Sheed & Ward, 1941.

Certain Difficulties Felt by Anglicans in Catholic Teaching, 1850. Reprint: London: Basil Montagu Pickering, 1876.

An Essay on the Development of Christian Doctrine, 1846. Reprint: edited by J. Cameron. Middlesex, England: Penguin Books, 1974.

An Essay in Aid of a Grammar of Assent, 1870. Reprint: Westminster, Md.: Christian Classics, 1973.

The Idea of the University: Defined and Illustrated. London: Longmans, Green & Co., 1927.

"The Infidelity of the Future." In *Faith and Prejudice and Other Unpublished Sermons of Cardinal Newman*. New York: Sheed & Ward, 1956.

The Letters and Diaries of John Henry Newman. Edited by Charles Stephen Dessain. London: Thomas Nelson and Sons, 1961.

Loss and Gain. Boston: Patrick Donahoe, 1854.

"The Newman–Perrone Paper on Development." *Gregorianum* XVI (1935): 402–447.

"Oratory Papers No. 36." In *Newman the Oratorian*. Edited by Placid Murray, O.S.B. Dublin: Gill and Macmillan Ltd., 1969. Pages 290–391.

Parochial and Plain Sermons. 8 volumes. New York: Longmans, Green & Co., 1907–1909.

"The Pillar of the Cloud." In *Verses on Various Occasions.* London: Burns and Oates, 1883.

Prayers, Verses, and Devotions. Reprint: San Francisco: Ignatius Press, 1989.

"The Second Spring." In *Sermons Preached on Various Occasions.* London: Longmans, Green & Co., 1892.

Sermons 1824–1843. Edited by Vincent Blehl, S.J. Oxford: Clarendon Press, 1993.

The Via Media of the Anglican Church. Vol. 1 in *Lectures of the Prophetical Office of the Church,* 1837. Reprint: Westminster, Md.: Christian Classics, 1978.

SECONDARY SOURCES

Antrobus, Frederick Ignatius. Preface to *The Life of Saint Philip Neri,* by Father P. G. Bacci. London: Kegan, Paul, Trench, Trubner, 1902.

Bacci, P. G. *The Life of Saint Philip Neri.* London: Kegan Paul, Trench, Trubner, 1902.

Barricelli, Gian Piero. *Alessandro Manzoni.* Boston: Twayne Publishers, 1976.

Biemer, Günter. *Newman on Tradition.* New York: Herder and Herder, 1967.

Bouyer, Louis. *Newman: His Life and Spirituality.* New York: P. J. Kennedy & Sons, 1958.

———. *St. Philip Neri: A Portrait.* Translated by Michael Day. London: Geoffrey Chapman, 1958.

Bozzetti, Giuseppe. Quoted in Claude Leetham, *Rosmini: Priest, Philosopher and Patriot.* London: Longmans, Green & Co., 1957. Pages xvi–xvii.

Butler, Joseph. *Analogy of Religion.* Quoted in Günter Biemer, *Newman on Tradition.* New York: Herder and Herder, 1967. Page 14.

Capecelatro, Alfonso Cardinale. "Commemorazione del Cardinale Enrico Newman." Speech given to the Confratelli dell'Oratorio di Napoli, 6 November 1890. Napoli: Tipografia dell'Accademia Reale delle Scienze, 1890.

Cerrato, Edoardo Aldo. "Saluto da Parte della Confederazione dell'Oratorio di San Filippo Neri." In *Conoscere Newman.* Città del Vaticano: Urbaniana University Press, 2002.

Church, Richard William. Quoted in C. S. Dessain, "Cardinal Newman's Attraction to St. Philip." *Oratorium* 1 (1970): 71.

————. Quoted in Charles Stephen Dessain, *John Henry Newman.* Stanford, Calif.: Stanford University Press, 1971. Page 89.

Cossiga, Francesco. "Newman the Man." In *Newman: A Man for Our Time.* Edited by David Brown. Harrisburg, Pa.: Morehouse Publishing, 1990.

Coulson, John. *Newman and the Common Tradition.* Oxford: Clarendon Press, 1970.

Davis, H. Francis. Foreword to *Newman on Tradition*, by Günter Biemer. New York: Herder and Herder, 1967.

De Liguori, St. Alphonsus. *Alphonsus de Liguori: Selected Writings.* Edited by Frederick M. Jones, C.SS.R. New York: Paulist Press, 1999.

Dessain, Charles Stephen. "Cardinal Newman's Attraction to St. Philip." *Oratorium* 1 (1970): 69–77.

————. *John Henry Newman.* Stanford, Calif.: Stanford University Press, 1971.

Ferreira, M. Jamie. *Doubt and Religious Commitment.* Oxford: Clarendon Press, 1980.

Flanagan, Philip. *Faith and the Believer.* London: Sands & Co., 1946.

Flynn, James. *Antonio Rosmini: Man of God.* No. 2. Rome: Collegio Rosmini, n.d.

Froude, Richard Hurrell. Quoted in *The Letters and Diaries of John Henry Newman.* Vol. 3, page 2.

Gilley, Sheridan. *Newman and His Age.* London: Darton, Longman and Todd, 1990.

Godt, Clareece G. *The Mobile Spectacle: Variable Perspective in Manzoni's "I Promessi Sposi."* New York: Peter Lang, 1998.

Graef, Hilda. *God and Myself: The Spirituality of John Henry Newman.* New York: Hawthorn Books, 1968.

Gregoris, Nicholas L. *"The Daughter of Eve Unfallen": Mary in the Theology and Spirituality of John Henry Newman.* Mount Pocono, Pa.: Newman House Press, 2003.

Gwynn, Denis. Quoted in *Dominic Barberi in England: A New Series of Letters.* London: Burns Oates & Washbourne, 1935.

———. *Father Dominic Barberi.* Buffalo, N.Y.: Desmond & Stapleton, 1948.

———. "Father Dominic Barberi and Cardinal Wiseman." *Westminster Cathedral Chronicle* 34 (1945): 177–181.

Harrold, Charles Frederick. *John Henry Newman.* London: Longmans, Green & Co., 1945.

Hollis, Christopher. *Newman and the Modern World.* Garden City, New York: Doubleday & Co., 1968.

Honoré, Jean Cardinal. *The Spiritual Journey of Newman.* New York: Alba House, 1992.

John Paul II, Pope. *Fides et Ratio: To the Bishops of the Catholic Church on the Relationship between Faith and Reason.* 15 September 1998.

Jones, Frederick M., C.SS.R., ed. *Alphonsus de Liguori: Selected Writings.* New York: Paulist Press, 1999.

Ker, Ian. Introduction to John Henry Newman, *Apologia pro Vita Sua: Being a History of His Religious Opinions.* Edited by Ian Ker. London: Penguin Books, 1994.

———. *The Catholic Revival in English Literature, 1845–1961.* Notre Dame, Ind.: University of Notre Dame Press, 2003.

———. *John Henry Newman: A Biography.* Oxford: Oxford University Press, 1988.

Lease, Gary. *Witness to the Faith.* Pittsburgh: Duquesne University Press, 1971.

Leetham, Claude. *Rosmini: Priest, Philosopher and Patriot.* London: Longmans, Green & Co., 1957.

Lynch, Rev. T. Introduction to "The Newman–Perrone Paper on Development." *Gregorianum* 16 (1935): 402–447.

Manning, Henry Edward. Quoted in *Dominic Barberi in England: A New Series of Letters*. Edited by Father Urban Young. London: Burns Oates & Washbourne, 1935.

Manzoni, Alessandro. *The Betrothed* [*I Promessi Sposi*]. Edited by Bruce Penman. London: Penguin Books, 1972.

May, J. Lewis. *Cardinal Newman*. Westminster, Md.: The Newman Press, 1971.

Moody, John. *John Henry Newman*. New York: Sheed & Ward, 1945.

Newman, Bertram. *Cardinal Newman: A Biographical and Literary Study*. London: G. Bell and Sons, 1925.

Nina, Lorenzo Cardinal. Quoted in *The Letters and Diaries of John Henry Newman*. Vol. 29, page 84.

Norris, Thomas J. *Newman and His Theological Method*. Leiden, Netherlands: E. J. Brill, 1977.

Paoli, Francesco. *Della Vita di Antonio Rosmini-Serbati*. Torino: Dall'Academia di Roverto, 1880.

Patrone, Antonio. "Rosmini–Newman: un incontro mancato tra due personalità filosofiche." *Oratorium* (1976), 53–66.

Penman, Bruce, translator and editor: Alessandro Manzoni, *The Betrothed* [*I Promessi Sposi*]. London: Penguin Books, 1972.

Perrone, Giovanni. In "The Newman–Perrone Paper on Development." Edited by Rev. T. Lynch. *Gregorianum* 16 (1935): 402–447.

———. *Praelectiones Theologicae*. Rome: Typis Collegii Urbani, 1840.

Ratzinger, Joseph Cardinal. "Note on the Force of the Doctrinal Decrees Concerning the Thought and Work of Father Antonio Rosmini Serbati." Internet database.

Rosmini, Antonio. *The Ascetical Letters*. Vol. 2. Loughborough, England: John Morris, Our Lady's Convent, 1995.

———. *Theological Language*. Translated by Denis Cleary. Durham, England: Rosmini House, 2004.

Sheridan, Thomas L., S.J. *Newman on Justification*. Staten Island, N.Y.: Society of St. Paul, 1967.

Slavin, Howard B., M.D. "Newman's Illness in Sicily: A Review and Interpretation." *Dublin Review* 238 (1964): 35–53.

St. John of Fawsley, Lord. "Newman: A Portrait." In *Newman: A Man for Our Time*. Edited by David Brown. Harrisburg, Pa.: Morehouse Publishing, 1990.

Strange, Roderick. "A Strange Providence: Newman's Illness in Sicily." *Louvain Studies* 15 (1990): 151–165.

Our Sunday Visitor's Catholic Encyclopedia. Edited by Rev. Peter M. J. Stravinskas. Huntington, Ind.: Our Sunday Visitor, 1991.

Tames, Richard. *A Traveller's History of Oxford*. New York: Interlink Books, 2003.

Tracey, Gerard. Quoted in *The Letters and Diaries of John Henry Newman*. Vol. 7, page 637.

Trevor, Meriol. *Newman's Journey*. Huntington, Ind.: Our Sunday Visitor, 1985.

———. *Newman: The Pillar of the Cloud*. Garden City, N.Y.: Doubleday, 1962.

Tristram, Henry. *Newman and His Friends*. London: John Lane, The Bodley Head, 1933.

Turks, Paul. *Philip Neri: The Fire of Joy*. Translated by Daniel Utrecht. New York: Alba House, 1995.

Velocci, Giovanni, C.SS.R. *Newman: Il Corraggio Della Verità*. Vatican City: Libreria Editrice Vaticana, 2000.

Wall, Bernard. *Alessandro Manzoni*. New Haven: Yale University Press, 1954.

Ward, Maisie. *Young Mr. Newman*. New York: Sheed & Ward, 1948.

Ward, Wilfred. *The Life of John Henry Newman*. 2 volumes. London: Longmans, Green & Co., 1912.

White, Joseph Blanco. Quoted in *The Letters and Diaries of John Henry Newman*. Vol. 3, page 351.

Winterton, Gregory. "Don't Forget Blessed Dominic." *Friends of Cardinal Newman Newsletter* (New Year, 2005). Page 10.

Young, Percy M. *Elgar, Newman and "The Dream of Gerontius."* Hants, England: Scolar Press, 1995.

Young, Urban, editor: *Dominic Barberi in England: A New Series of Letters.* London: Burns Oates & Washbourne, 1935.

Made in the USA
Charleston, SC
29 January 2010